Raspberry Pi Computer Vision Programming

Design and implement your own computer vision applications with the Raspberry Pi

Ashwin Pajankar

BIRMINGHAM - MUMBAI

Raspberry Pi Computer Vision Programming

First published: May 2015

Production reference: 1250515

Published by Packt Publishing Ltd.
Livery Place
35 Livery Street
Birmingham B3 2PB, UK.

ISBN 978-1-78439-828-6

www.packtpub.com

Credits

Author
Ashwin Pajankar

Reviewers
James Allen
Arush Kakkar
Luis A. Larco
Fred Stakem
Aldo Vargas

Commissioning Editor
Amit Ghodake

Acquisition Editor
Llewellyn Rozario

Content Development Editor
Merwyn D'souza

Technical Editor
Edwin Moses

Copy Editors
Puja Lalwani
Vedangi Narvekar

Project Coordinator
Nikhil Nair

Proofreaders
Stephen Copestake
Safis Editing

Indexer
Priya Sane

Graphics
Sheetal Aute
Disha Haria

Production Coordinator
Shantanu Zagade

Cover Work
Shantanu Zagade

About the Author

Ashwin Pajankar is a Bangalore-based software professional with more than 5 years of experience in software design, development, testing, and automation. He graduated from IIT Hyderabad with an MTech degree in computer science and engineering. He holds multiple professional certifications from Oracle, IBM, Teradata, and ISTQB in development, databases, and testing. Apart from work, he enjoys serving the community. He has won several awards in college through college outreach initiatives and at work for community service through his employers for corporate social responsibility programs. He was introduced to the Raspberry Pi while organizing a hackathon at his workplace, and he's been hooked on to Pi ever since. He writes plenty of code in Bash, Python, and Java on his cluster of Pi. Currently, he's building India's biggest cluster of the recently launched Raspberry Pi 2. He's reviewed two other titles related to Python from Packt and is working on another book on Raspberry Pi.

You can view Ashwin's LinkedIn profile by visiting `in.linkedin.com/in/ashwinpajankar`.

I would like to thank my wife, Kavitha, for motivating me to write this book to share my knowledge with others. I would also like to thank Merwyn D'Souza and Llewellyn Rozario from Packt Publishing for providing me with the opportunity, guidance, and necessary support to write this book. Last but not least, I would like to thank all the reviewers who helped me make the book better by providing their precious feedback.

About the Reviewers

James Allen is a computer scientist and a teacher whose experiences run the gamut from web and application programming to graphic design and sound engineering. If a form of media can be produced on a computer, there is a very good chance that he has dabbled in something along those lines.

He is very interested in the enabling factor of technology and how advancements in personal computers and handheld devices have opened up a wide variety of activities to a big chunk of the population. He is especially interested in opening up these activities further. Above all, he wants to be happy and bring happiness to others. You can read more about his (mis)adventures by visiting `http://jamesmallen.net`.

Arush Kakkar is a robotics enthusiast who has experience in computer vision, machine learning, and hardware technologies. His primary focus is on autonomous robotics, which includes drones and self-driving cars. He has contributed to the development of these systems in different capacities, including computer vision and path planning. He is the electronics engineer for the solar car team of his university, DTU Solaris. He is also interested in building commercial solutions in robotics to reduce the manual labor required in jobs. You can contact him through his website, `www.arushkakkar.com`, and read about some of his projects on `http://blog.arushkakkar.com`.

Luis A. Larco is a software engineer at GE Healthcare in Milwaukee, Wisconsin, as well as a research associate at the Medical Imaging Research Center (MIRC) at the Illinois Institute of Technology in Chicago, Illinois. Originally from Lima, Peru, Luis was raised in Miami, Florida, where he attended high school and college. He subsequently relocated to Illinois and studied at the Illinois Institute of Technology. He received bachelor's degrees in electrical engineering and computer engineering. While studying for his undergraduate degree, he worked on a research project with the Chicago Police Department on predictive policing. In his free time, he enjoys performing with his jazz band, where he plays the bass, as well as hiking and mountain biking.

Aldo Vargas is a mechatronics engineer who graduated from UNAM in Mexico City. He has previously worked in the robotics industry. He is currently completing his PhD in aerospace engineering from the University of Glasgow, United Kingdom. He is developing GNC (guidance, navigation, and control) algorithms for unmanned aerial systems. The research aim is to give UAS the ability to "see" using advanced and practical computer vision algorithms programmed in Python. He has academic and industrial experience in control systems, embedded systems, artificial intelligence, machine learning, computer vision, robotics, and systems integration.

Aldo loves to design, build, and control drones at work and during his free time. He also enjoys scuba diving, skydiving, and riding motorcycles. If you're interested in knowing more about his work, you can visit `http://aldux.net`.

www.PacktPub.com

Support files, eBooks, discount offers, and more

For support files and downloads related to your book, please visit www.PacktPub.com.

Did you know that Packt offers eBook versions of every book published, with PDF and ePub files available? You can upgrade to the eBook version at www.PacktPub.com and as a print book customer, you are entitled to a discount on the eBook copy. Get in touch with us at service@packtpub.com for more details.

At www.PacktPub.com, you can also read a collection of free technical articles, sign up for a range of free newsletters and receive exclusive discounts and offers on Packt books and eBooks.

https://www2.packtpub.com/books/subscription/packtlib

Do you need instant solutions to your IT questions? PacktLib is Packt's online digital book library. Here, you can search, access, and read Packt's entire library of books.

Why subscribe?

- Fully searchable across every book published by Packt
- Copy and paste, print, and bookmark content
- On demand and accessible via a web browser

Free access for Packt account holders

If you have an account with Packt at www.PacktPub.com, you can use this to access PacktLib today and view 9 entirely free books. Simply use your login credentials for immediate access.

Table of Contents

Preface

Raspberry Pi was developed as a low-cost single-board computer with the intention of promoting computer science education in schools. It also represents a welcome return to a simple and fun yet effective way to learn computer science and programming.

You can use Raspberry Pi to learn and implement concepts in computer vision.

With a $35 Raspberry Pi computer and a USB webcam, anyone can afford to become a pro in computer vision in no time and build a real-life computer vision application to impress friends and colleagues.

What this book covers

Chapter 1, Introduction to Computer Vision and Raspberry Pi, takes you through the introduction and initial setup of Raspberry Pi and computer vision.

Chapter 2, Working with Images, Webcams, and GUI, teaches you how to work with images, videos, and various cameras.

Chapter 3, Basic Image Processing, explores arithmetic and logical operations on images.

Chapter 4, Colorspaces, Transformations, and Thresholds, introduces you to colorspaces and conversions, which are then followed by a simple project. This chapter also explores geometric transformations and segmentation by thresholding.

Chapter 5, Let's Make Some Noise, teaches the basics of noise in digital images and low-pass filters. It also discussed their usage in the removal of noise from images.

Chapter 6, Edges, Circles, and Lines' Detection, explores high-pass filters and their applications. It also explores the detection of features like edges, circles, and lines.

Chapter 7, Image Restoration, Quantization, and Depth Map, explores image restoration by inpainting. It also teaches image segmentation, quantization, and depth maps.

Chapter 8, Histograms, Contours, Morphological Transformations, and Performance Measurement, introduces the readers to histograms and plotting. It explores the concepts of contours and morphological transformations on an image. It concludes with the basics of performance measurement and improvement.

Chapter 9, Real-life Computer Vision Applications, implements various real-life applications of computer vision using Raspberry Pi and a webcam.

Chapter 10, Introduction to SimpleCV, teaches the installation and usage of SimpleCV, a powerful yet simple computer vision library, and concludes with a few real-life projects.

What you need for this book

The following hardware is recommended for maximum enjoyment:

- The Raspberry Pi computer (Model B, B+, or Pi 2)
- SD card (8 GB minimum)
- 5V 1A power supply
- HDMI or VGA monitor
- HDMI to VGA converter if a VGA monitor is used
- Wired Internet connection
- A keyboard and a mouse
- A good quality webcam
- A Pi Camera
- A Windows computer/laptop with an embedded or external card reader

Who this book is for

This book is intended for novices as well as seasoned Raspberry Pi and Python enthusiasts who would like to explore the area of computer vision. Readers with very little programming or coding/scripting experience can create wonderful image processing and computer vision applications with relatively few lines of code in Python.

Conventions

In this book, you will find a number of text styles that distinguish between different kinds of information. Here are some examples of these styles and an explanation of their meaning.

Code words in text, database table names, folder names, filenames, file extensions, pathnames, dummy URLs, user input, and Twitter handles are shown as follows: " We are going to learn about the `linspace()` function now."

A block of code is set as follows:

```
import picamera
import time

with picamera.PiCamera() as cam:
  cam.resolution=(1024,768)
  cam.start_preview()
  time.sleep(5)
  cam.capture('/home/pi/book/output/still.jpg')
```

Any command-line input or output is written as follows:

```
>>> a**2
array([ 1,  9, 36, 81])
```

New terms and **important words** are shown in bold. Words that you see on the screen, for example, in menus or dialog boxes, appear in the text like this: "Go to **Enable Boot to Desktop/Scratch | Desktop.**"

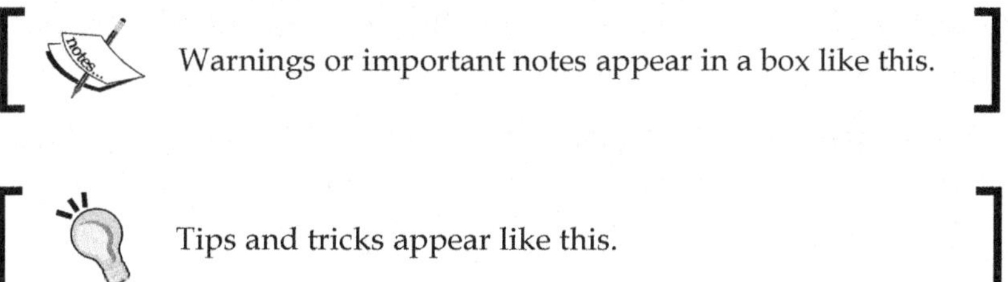

Reader feedback

Feedback from our readers is always welcome. Let us know what you think about this book—what you liked or disliked. Reader feedback is important for us as it helps us develop titles that you will really get the most out of.

To send us general feedback, simply e-mail `feedback@packtpub.com`, and mention the book's title in the subject of your message.

If there is a topic that you have expertise in and you are interested in either writing or contributing to a book, see our author guide at `www.packtpub.com/authors`.

Customer support

Now that you are the proud owner of a Packt book, we have a number of things to help you to get the most from your purchase.

Downloading the example code

You can download the example code files from your account at `http://www.packtpub.com` for all the Packt Publishing books you have purchased. If you purchased this book elsewhere, you can visit `http://www.packtpub.com/support` and register to have the files e-mailed directly to you.

Errata

Although we have taken every care to ensure the accuracy of our content, mistakes do happen. If you find a mistake in one of our books—maybe a mistake in the text or the code—we would be grateful if you could report this to us. By doing so, you can save other readers from frustration and help us improve subsequent versions of this book. If you find any errata, please report them by visiting `http://www.packtpub.com/submit-errata`, selecting your book, clicking on the **Errata Submission Form** link, and entering the details of your errata. Once your errata are verified, your submission will be accepted and the errata will be uploaded to our website or added to any list of existing errata under the Errata section of that title.

To view the previously submitted errata, go to `https://www.packtpub.com/books/content/support` and enter the name of the book in the search field. The required information will appear under the **Errata** section.

Piracy

Piracy of copyrighted material on the Internet is an ongoing problem across all media. At Packt, we take the protection of our copyright and licenses very seriously. If you come across any illegal copies of our works in any form on the Internet, please provide us with the location address or website name immediately so that we can pursue a remedy.

Please contact us at `copyright@packtpub.com` with a link to the suspected pirated material.

We appreciate your help in protecting our authors and our ability to bring you valuable content.

Questions

If you have a problem with any aspect of this book, you can contact us at `questions@packtpub.com`, and we will do our best to address the problem.

1
Introduction to Computer Vision and Raspberry Pi

OpenCV is a simple yet powerful tool for any computer vision enthusiast. One can learn computer vision in an easy way by writing OpenCV programs in Python. The Raspberry Pi family of single-board computers uses Python as the preferred development platform. Using a Raspberry Pi computer and Python for OpenCV programming is one of the best ways to start your journey into the world of computer vision. We will commence our journey with this chapter by getting ourselves familiar with the following topics:

- Computer vision
- OpenCV
- Raspberry Pi
- Setting up Raspberry Pi
- Installing OpenCV and its dependencies
- NumPy basics

Computer vision

Computer vision is an area of computer science, mathematics, and electrical engineering. It includes ways to acquire, process, analyze, and understand images and videos from the real world in order to mimic human vision. Also, unlike human vision, computer vision can also be used to analyze and process depth and infrared images.

Computer vision is also concerned with the theory of information extraction from images and videos. A computer vision system can accept different forms of data as an input, including, but not limited to, images, image sequences, and videos that can be streamed from multiple sources to further process and extract useful information from for decision making.

Artificial intelligence and computer vision share many topics, such as image processing, pattern recognition, and machine learning techniques, as shown in the following diagram:

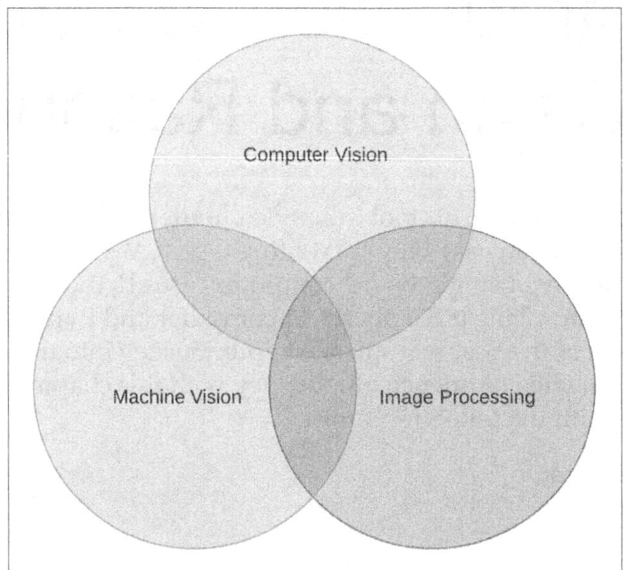

The typical tasks of computer vision include the following:

- Object recognition and classification
- Motion detection and analysis
- Image and scene reconstruction

Don't worry about this jargon as of now. We will explore most of these concepts in detail in the later chapters.

OpenCV

OpenCV (**Open Source ComputerVision**) is a library of programming functions for computer vision. It was initially developed by the Intel Russia research center in Nizhny Novgorod, and it is currently maintained by Itseez.

You can read more about Itseez at `http://itseez.com/`.

This is a cross-platform library, which means that it can be implemented and operated on different operating systems. It focuses mainly on image and video processing. In addition to this, it has several GUI and event handling features for the user's convenience.

OpenCV was released under a **Berkeley Software Distribution** (**BSD**) license and hence, it is free for both academic and commercial use. It has interfaces for popular programming languages, such as C/C++, Python, and Java, and it runs on a variety of operating systems including Windows, Android, and Unix-like operating systems.

You can explore the OpenCV homepage, `www.opencv.org`, for further details.

OpenCV was initially an Intel Research initiative to develop tools to analyze images.

Following is the timeline of OpenCV in brief:

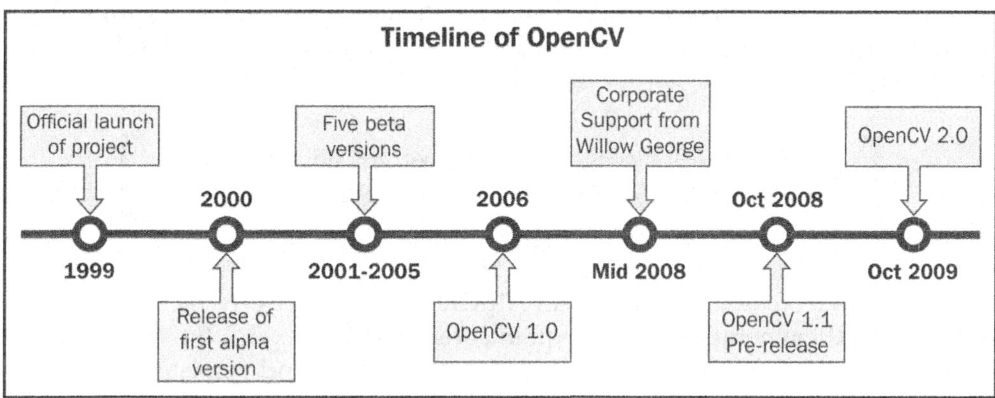

In August 2012, support for OpenCV was taken over by a nonprofit foundation, OpenCV.org, which is currently developing it further. It also maintains a developer and user site for OpenCV.

At the time of writing this book, the stable version of OpenCV was 2.4.10. Version 3.0 Beta is also available.

Single-board computers and the Raspberry Pi

A single-board computer system is a complete computer on a single board. The board includes processor(s), RAM, I/O, and networking ports for interfacing devices. Unlike traditional computer systems, single-board computers are not modular and its hardware cannot be upgraded as it's integrated on the board itself. Single-board computers are used as low-cost computers in academic and research settings. The use of single-board computers in embedded systems is very prevalent, and many individuals and organizations have developed and released fully functional products based on single-board computers.

Popular single-board computers available in the market include, but are not limited to, Raspberry Pi, Banana Pi, BeagleBone, and Cubieboard.

Raspberry Pi

Raspberry Pi is a series of low-cost, palm-sized, single-board computers developed by the Raspberry Pi Foundation in the UK. The intention behind the creation of Raspberry Pi was to promote the teaching of basic computer skills in schools, and the former serves this purpose well. Raspberry Pi has expanded its footprint well beyond its intended purpose by penetrating into the market of embedded systems and research.

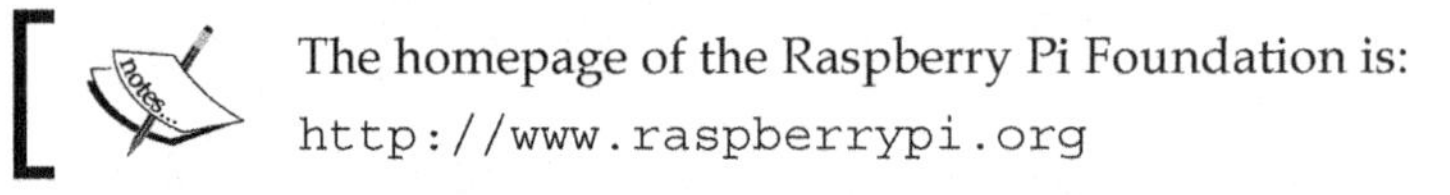

The homepage of the Raspberry Pi Foundation is: `http://www.raspberrypi.org`

Raspberry Pi models—A, A+, B, and B+—are based on SoC (system on a chip) Broadcom BCM2835, which includes an ARM11 700 MHz CPU (which can be overclocked). RPi generation 2 uses a quad core ARM Cortex-A7, the first multicore Raspberry Pi. Raspberry Pi A and B use SD cards for boot and persistent storage, whereas models A+, B+, and Pi 2 use microSD cards for the same. The models A and A+ have 256 MB of RAM, B and B+ have 512 MB of RAM, and Pi 2 has 1 GB of RAM.

As of now, there are five major models of Raspberry Pi, which are as follows:

- Model A
- Model A+ (currently in production and available for purchase)
- Model B (available for purchase but not in production)

- Model B+ (currently in production and available for purchase)
- Raspberry Pi 2 (currently in production and available for purchase)

Check out the product page of Raspberry Pi at the following location: http://www.raspberrypi.org/products/

The Raspberry Pi Foundation provides Debian and Arch variants and Linux ARM distributions for download. Python is the main programming platform and languages like C, C++, Java, Perl, and Ruby can be used to program Raspberry Pi.

We will use Raspberry Pi B+ for our Computer Vision learning. However, these examples can also be executed on other Raspberry Pi Models.

The Raspberry Pi B+ specifications are as follows:

Component	Specification
CPU	700 MHz ARM1176JZF-S core (ARM11 family, ARM v6 instruction set)
GPU	Broadcom VideoCore IV @250 MHz
Memory	512 MB SDRAM (shared with GPU – the limit of memory used by GPU can be set using `raspi-config` utility)
USB 2.0 ports	4
Video output	HDMI, composite video (PAL and NTSC) via 3.5 mm TRRS jack shared with audio out (you need to use converters for VGA type displays)
Audio output	Analog via 3.5 mm phone jack; digital via HDMI port
Onboard storage	microSD
Networking	10/100 Mbit/s Fast Ethernet, no onboard Wi-Fi or Bluetooth
Power	600 mA (3 W), 5 V via `http://en.wikipedia.org/wiki/MicroUSB` or GPIO header (using MicroUSB for power is recommended)

Operating systems

Raspberry Pi primarily uses Unix-like, Linux-kernel-based operating systems, like the variants of Debian and Fedora.

The Raspberry Pi models A, A+, B, and B+ are based on the ARM11 family chip, which runs on the ARM v6 instruction set. The ARM v6 instruction set does not support Ubuntu and Windows.

However, the recently launched Raspberry Pi 2 is based on ARM Cortex A7, which is capable of running both Windows 10 and Ubuntu (Snappy Core). The following operating systems are officially supported by all the models of Raspberry Pi and are available for download at the download page:

- OpenELEC
- Pidora (Fedora Remix)
- RASPBMC
- RISC OS
- Raspbian—we will use this with a Raspberry Pi B+ throughout this book.

Windows 10 and Ubuntu are supported by only the recently launched Pi 2.

Raspbian

Raspbian is an unofficial variant of Debian Wheezy **armhf** (**ARM hard float**) that is compiled for hard float code that will run on Raspberry Pi computers. It is a free operating system based on Debian that is optimized for the Raspberry Pi hardware. Raspbian is more than a pure OS. It comes with over 35,000 packages and precompiled software for Raspberry Pi.

To know more about Raspbian, you can visit `http://www.raspbian.org/`.

Setting up your Raspberry Pi B+

This is the front view of Raspberry Pi B+:

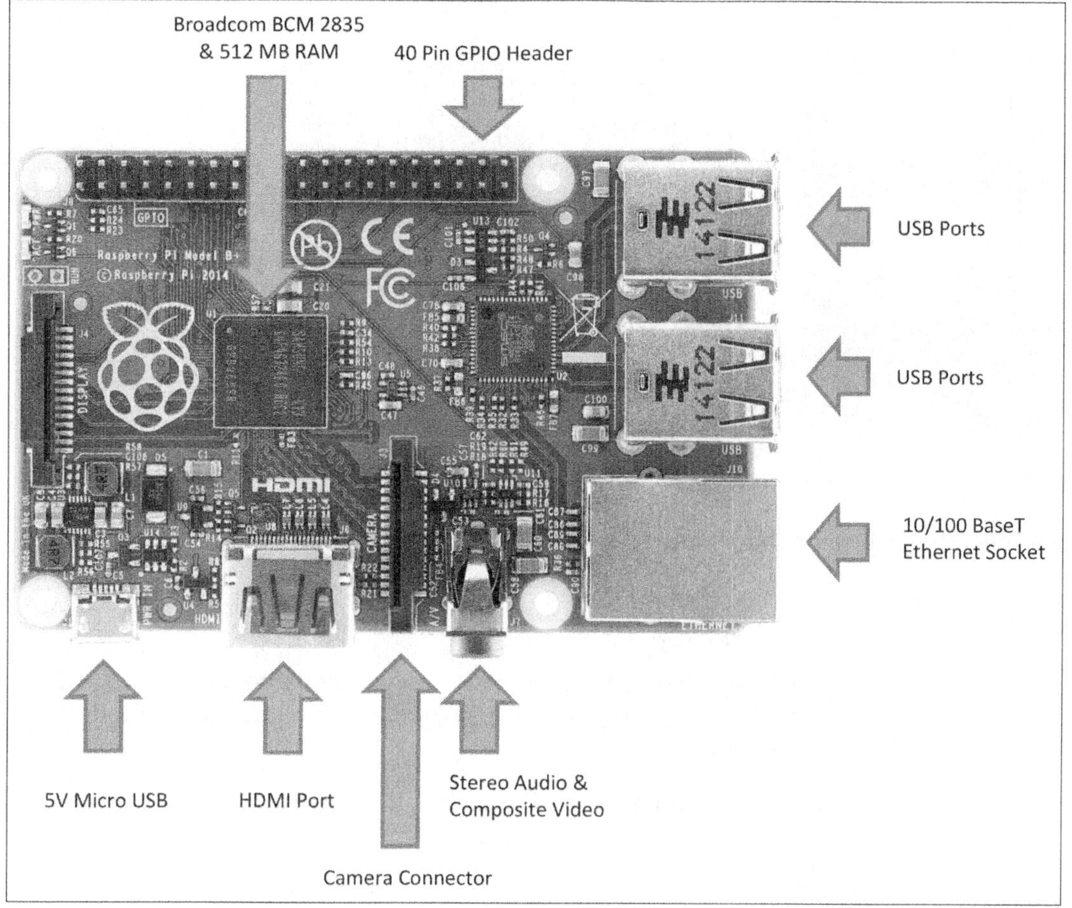

This is the flipside of Raspberry Pi B+:

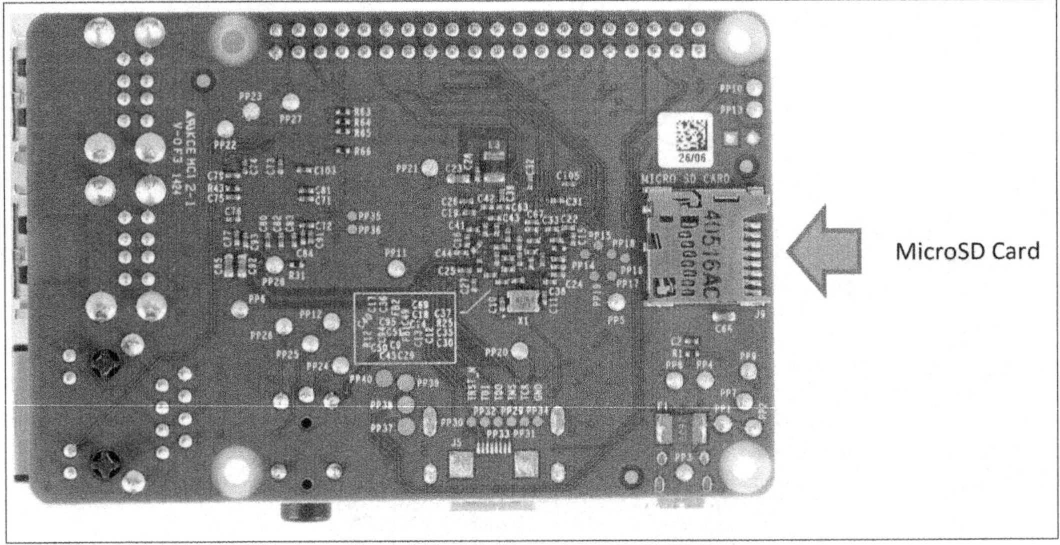

We need the following hardware to set up a Pi:

- Raspberry Pi B+
- A micro USB power supply

  Considering that we are going for a bit of power-intensive usage for our Pi B+ (like connecting picamera), a 5V 2A power supply is recommended.
- A standard USB keyboard
- A microSD card and a microSD to SD card converter

  We need a microSD card of minimum 4 GB.
- A USB mouse
- A monitor

  You can either use an HDMI monitor or a standard VGA monitor.
- A monitor connection cable and a converter

  If you are using an HDMI Monitor, then an HDMI cable is sufficient.
  If you are using a VGA monitor, then you need to use an HDMI to VGA converter with a VGA cable. A few special changes should be made to `/boot/config.txt` if you're using a VGA monitor, which will be explained in the next section.
- A Windows computer with a microSD card reader and a wired Internet connection

Preparing your microSD card manually

This is the original way of installing an OS into a microSD card, and many users, including me, still prefer it. It allows the SD card to be prepared manually before it is used, and it allows you to have easier access to the configuration files like `/boot/config.txt`, which might have to be modified in a few cases before booting up the system. The default Raspbian image consists of only two partitions—**boot** and **system**. These would fit into a 2 GB card. However, I recommend you to use a minimum 4 GB card to be on the safe side. Choosing an 8 GB card will be adequate for most of the applications.

Following are the instructions for the Windows users:

1. Download the installable file of Win32DiskImager that is available at `http://sourceforge.net/projects/win32diskimager/files/latest/download` and then install it.
2. Download the installable version of WinZip that is available at `http://www.winzip.com/prod_down.html%20` and install it.
3. Go to `http://www.raspberrypi.org/downloads` and download the latest image of Raspbian. It will be a compressed file in the ZIP format, and it needs to be extracted.
4. Extract the ZIP file using WinZip. The extracted file will be in the `img` format.
5. Insert your microSD card into the card reader and plug the card reader into your computer. Nowadays, many computers have an inbuilt SD card reader. In this case, you need to insert the microSD card into the microSD to SD card converter and insert that into your computer's inbuilt card reader.
6. Run the `Win32DiskImager.exe` file and write the image into your SD card.

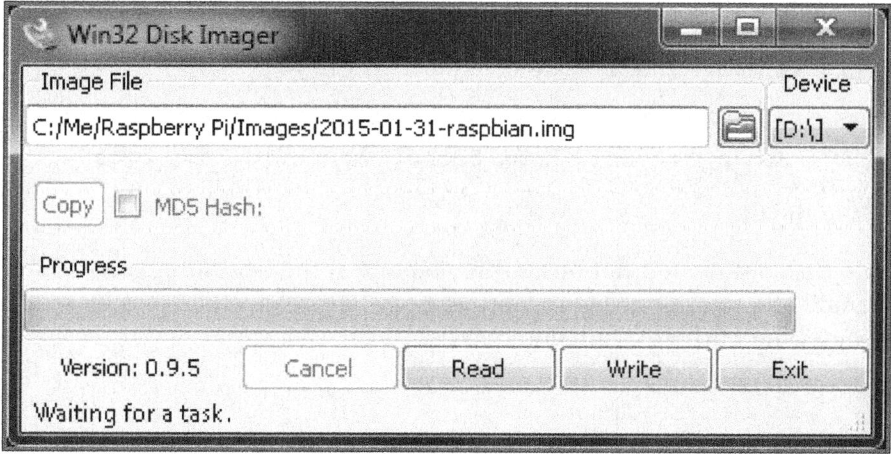

7. If you have an HDMI monitor, then please skip this step. This additional step is required only if you are planning to use a VGA monitor in place of an HDMI monitor.

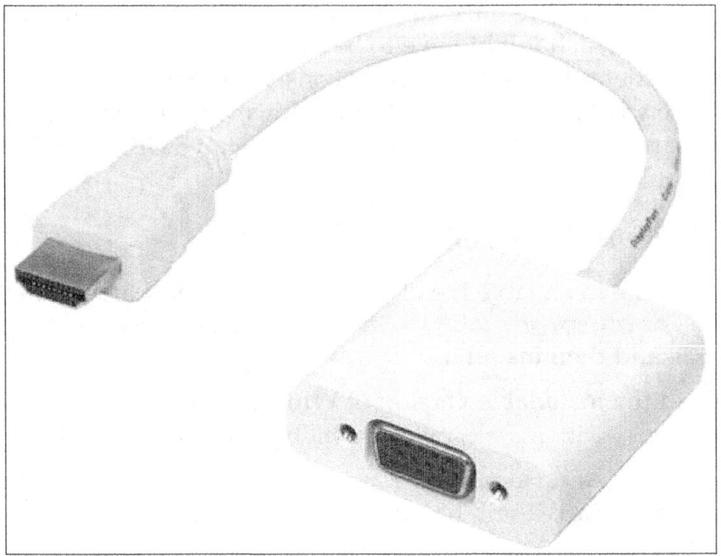

8. Browse the SD card. It will appear as a drive labeled `boot` in the Windows file explorer. Open the `config.txt` file from the explorer. You will have to edit the file in the following manner to enable a proper display on your VGA monitor
    - Change `#disable_overscan=1` to `disable_overscan=1`
    - Change `#hdmi_force_hotplug=1` to `hdmi_force_hotplug=1`
    - Change `#hdmi_group=1` to `hdmi_group=2`
    - Change `#hdmi_mode=1` to `hdmi_mode=16`
    - Change `#hdmi_drive=2` to `hdmi_drive=2`
    - Change `#config_hdmi_boost=4` to `config_hdmi_boost=4`
9. Save the file.

By default, the commented options (which have # at the beginning) are disabled. We will enable these options by uncommenting their respective lines by removing # at the beginning of these commented lines.

If you are using Linux or Mac OS, then you will find the instructions to install the OS on your Micro SD card for these operating systems at `https://www.raspberrypi.org/documentation/installation/installing-images/`.

Booting up your Raspberry Pi for the first time

Let's boot up our Pi for the first time with the microSD card in the following way:

1. Insert the microSD card into the microSD card slot of Pi.
2. Connect the Pi to the HDMI monitor. In case you have connected the VGA monitor, connect it using the HDMI to VGA converter.
3. Connect the USB mouse and USB keyboard.
4. Connect the Pi to the power supply with a micro USB power cable. Make sure that the power is switched off at this point.
5. Check all the connections once and then switch on the power supply of Pi.

At this stage, your Pi will start booting up. You will see a green light blinking on the Pi board. It means that it's working! Now, there are a few more things that you need to do before you can really start using your Pi. Once it boots up, it will show the `raspi-config` menu, as follows:

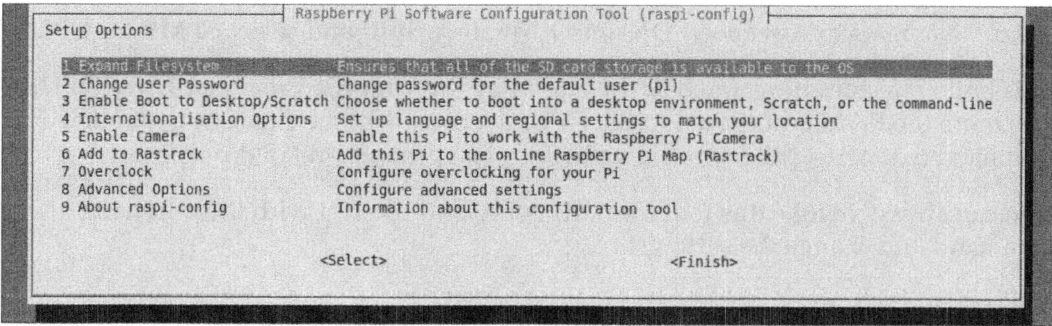

Perform the following steps and reboot the Pi at the end:

You will have to use the arrow keys and the *Enter* key to select options in the text-based menu.

1. Use **Expand Filesystem**.
2. Go to **Enable Boot to Desktop/Scratch** | **Desktop**. Log in as `pi` at the graphical desktop.

If you do not enable this option, you will be asked for the username and password every time you boot. The default username is `pi` and the password is `raspberry`. Once you enter the username and password, the command prompt will appear. The default shell of Raspbian is bash. You can confirm it by typing this in the following command:

```
echo $SHELL
```

You can always go to the graphical desktop by typing in the `startx` command. To use OpenCV with Python, we are required to use the GUI of Raspbian to display images and video.

3. Navigate to **Internationalisation Options** | **Change Keyboard Layout**. Change it to **US** (the default is UK).
4. Enable Camera.
5. Navigate to **Advanced Options** | **Memory Split** and select **64 MB** for GPU.

This option decides how much RAM is used by the **Graphic Processor Unit** (**GPU**). The more the RAM is allocated to the GPU, the more will the processing of intensive graphics be done. 64 MB is a good value for most graphics-related purposes.

You can always invoke this tool from the command prompt with the following command and change the settings:

```
sudo raspi-config
```

Shutting down and rebooting your Pi safely

In the Raspbian GUI, there are options that allow you to shut down and reboot Pi. From the command prompt, you can shut down Pi safely by issuing the following command:

```
sudo shutdown -h now
```

An alternative command is as follows:

```
sudo halt
```

You can reboot Pi by using the following command:

```
sudo reboot
```

Preparing your Pi for computer vision

Now, we have a working Pi running the Raspbian OS. Please make sure that you have a working wired Internet connection with a reasonable speed for this activity. Let's prepare Pi for computer vision:

1. Connect your Pi to an Internet modem or router with an Ethernet cable.
2. Run the following command to restart the networking service:
   ```
   sudo service networking restart
   ```
3. Make sure that Raspberry Pi is connected to the Internet by typing in the following command:
   ```
   ping -c4 www.google.com
   ```
4. Run the following commands in a sequence:

   Advanced Package Tool (apt) is the utility that can be used to install and remove software in Debian and its variants. We need to use it to update the Pi software.

   - `sudo apt-get update`

   This command synchronizes the package list from the source. Indexes of all the packages are refreshed. This command must be issued before we issue the upgrade command.

   - `sudo apt-get upgrade`

   This will install the newest versions of the already installed software. Obsolete packages/utilities are not removed automatically. If the software is up to date, then it's left as it is.

   - `sudo rpi-update`

   This command is used to upgrade the firmware. The kernel and firmware are installed as a Debian package, and hence, we will also get the updates. These packages are updated infrequently after extensive testing.

5. Now, we will need to install a few necessary packages and dependencies for OpenCV. Following is a list of packages we need to install. You just need to connect Pi to the Internet and type in sudo apt-get install <package-name>, where <package-name> is one of following packages:

libopencv-dev	libpng3	libdc1394-22-dev
build-essential	libpnglite-dev	libdc1394-22
libavformat-dev	zlib1g-dbg	libdc1394-utils
x264	zlib1g	libv4l-0
v4l-utils	zlib1g-dev	libv4l-dev
ffmpeg	pngtools	libpython2.6
libcv2.3	libtiff4-dev	python-dev
libcvaux2.3	libtiff4	python2.6-dev
libhighgui2.3	libtiffxx0c2	libgtk2.0-dev
python-opencv	libtiff-tools	libpngwriter0-dev
opencv-doc	libjpeg8	libpngwriter0c2
libcv-dev	libjpeg8-dev	libswscale-dev
libcvaux-dev	libjpeg8-dbg	libjpeg-dev
libhighgui-dev	libavcodec-dev	libwebp-dev
python-numpy	libavcodec53	libpng-dev
python-scipy	libavformat53	libtiff5-dev
python-matplotlib	libgstreamer0.10-0-dbg	libjasper-dev
python-pandas	libgstreamer0.10-0	libopenexr-dev
python-nose	libgstreamer0.10-dev	libgdal-dev
v4l-utils	libxine1-ffmpeg	python-tk
libgtkglext1-dev	libxine-dev	python3-dev
libpng12-0	libxine1-bin	python3-tk
libpng12-dev	libunicap2	python3-numpy
libpng++-dev	libunicap2-dev	libeigen3-dev

For example, if you want to install x264, you have to type `sudo apt-get install x264`. This will install the necessary package. Similarly, you can install all of the aforementioned packages in like manner. If a package is already installed on Pi, it will show the following message:

```
pi@pi02 ~ $ sudo apt-get install x264
Reading package lists... Done
Building dependency tree
Reading state information... Done
x264 is already the newest version.
0 upgraded, 0 newly installed, 0 to remove and 0 not
  upgraded.
```

In such cases, don't worry. The package you wanted to install has already been installed, and it is up to date. Just proceed with the installation of all the other packages in the list one-by-one.

6. Finally, install OpenCV for Python by using the following command:

   ```
   sudo apt-get install python-opencv
   ```

   This is the easiest way to install OpenCV for Python. However, there is a problem with this. Raspbian repositories may not always contain the latest version of OpenCV. For example, at the time of writing this book, Raspbian repository contains version 2.4.1, while the latest OpenCV version is 2.4.10. With respect to Python API, the latest version will always contain much better support and more functionality.

   Another method is to compile OpenCV from the source, which I will not recommend for beginners as it's a bit complex and it will take a lot of time.

Testing OpenCV installation with Python

It's very easy to code for OpenCV in Python. It requires very few lines of code compared to C/C++, and powerful libraries like NumPy can be exploited for multidimensional data structures that are required for image processing.

On a terminal, type `python`, and then type the following lines:

```
>>> import cv2
>>> print cv2.__version__
```

This will show us the version of OpenCV that was installed on Pi, which, in our case is 2.4.1.

NumPy

NumPy is a fundamental package that can be used to scientifically compute with Python. It is a matrix library for linear algebra. NumPy can also be used as an efficient multidimensional container of generic data. Arbitrary data types can be defined and used. NumPy is an extension of the Python programming language. It adds support for large multidimensional arrays and matrices, along with a large library of high-level mathematical functions that can be used to operate on these arrays. We will use NumPy arrays throughout this book to represent images and carry out complex mathematical operations. NumPy comes with many inbuilt functions for all of these operations. So, we do not have to worry about basic array operations. We can directly focus on the concepts and code for computer vision. All the OpenCV array structures are converted to and from NumPy arrays. So, whatever operations you perform in NumPy, you can combine NumPy with OpenCV.

We will use NumPy with OpenCV a lot in this book. Let's start with some simple example programs that will demonstrate the real power of NumPy.

Open Python via the terminal. Try the following examples.

Array creation

Let's see some examples on array creation. The `array()` method is used very frequently in this book. There are many ways to create different types of arrays. We will explore these ways as and when they are needed in this book. Follow these commands for array creation:

```
>>> import numpy as np
>>> x=np.array([1,2,3])
>>> x
array([1, 2, 3])

>>> y=arange(10)
>>> y
array([0, 1, 2, 3, 4, 5, 6, 7, 8, 9])
```

Basic operations on arrays

We are going to learn about the `linspace()` function now. It takes three parameters—`start_num`, `end_num`, and `count`. This creates an array with equally spaced points, starting from `start_num` and ending with `end_num`. You can try out the following example:

```
>>> a=np.array([1,3,6,9])
>>> b=np.linspace(0,15,4)
>>> c=a-b
>>> c
array([ 1., -2., -4., -6.])
```

Following is the code that can be used to calculate the square of every element in an array:

```
>>> a**2
array([ 1,  9, 36, 81])
```

Linear algebra

Let's explore some examples with regard to linear algebra. You will learn how to use the `transpose()`, `inv()`, `solve()`, and `dot()` functions, which are useful while performing operations related to linear algebra:

```
>>> a=np.array([[1,2,3],[4,5,6],[7,8,9]])
>>> a.transpose()
array([[1, 4, 7],
       [2, 5, 8],
       [3, 6, 9]])

>>> np.linalg.inv(a)
array([[ -4.50359963e+15,   9.00719925e+15,  -4.50359963e+15],
       [  9.00719925e+15,  -1.80143985e+16,   9.00719925e+15],
       [ -4.50359963e+15,   9.00719925e+15,  -4.50359963e+15]])
```

```
>>> b=np.array([3,2,1])
>>> np.linalg.solve(a,b)
array([ -9.66666667,  15.33333333,  -6.        ])

>>> c=np.random.rand(3,3)
>>> c
array([[ 0.69551123,  0.18417943,  0.0298238 ],
       [ 0.11574883,  0.39692914,  0.93640691],
       [ 0.36908272,  0.53802672,  0.2333465 ]])
>>> np.dot(a,c)
array([[ 2.03425705,  2.59211786,  2.60267713],
       [ 5.57528539,  5.94952371,  6.20140877],
       [ 9.11631372,  9.30692956,  9.80014041]])
```

You can explore NumPy in detail at `http://www.numpy.org/`.

Summary

In this chapter, we learned about the background of OpenCV, Raspberry Pi, and computer vision. We learned how to set up Raspberry Pi to program computer vision with OpenCV. We also went through some examples on NumPy.

In the next chapter, we will learn how to work with images, videos, webcam, and the Pi camera.

2
Working with Images, Webcams, and GUI

In our last chapter, we discovered how to set up Pi for OpenCV programming. In this chapter, we will start with writing snippets of code for images and video, GUI, and cameras. Let's take a look at the topics we will cover in this chapter:

- Working with images
- Drawing functions and trackbar
- Webcam and videos
- Picamera

Running Python programs with Raspberry Pi

In our last chapter, we saw how to use the Python interpreter to run Python commands. However, for the next programs, we will be running Python scripts instead. We will have to run these programs from LXTerminal. There are three ways to open LXTerminal:

- The desktop usually comes with an icon to access the LXTerminal. Click on that icon to open it.
- If the icon is not on the desktop, you will find it under **Accessories** in **Menu**.
- As a shortcut, you can press *Alt* + *F2* and type `lxterminal`. This will invoke the program directly. This method might be useful in case you do not have a mouse available.

Once you open LXTerminal, you will see a prompt similar to the following one:

```
pi@pi02 ~ $
```

Here, `pi` is the user and `pi02` is the hostname. The hostname can be set by invoking `raspi-config`. I have set the name as `pi02` as it is the second node of my three-node Raspberry Pi B+ cluster. For simplicity, you can set your own name as the hostname. For example, if you set your hostname as `ashwin`, the prompt will appear as follows:

```
pi@ashwin ~ $
```

It is recommended that you create a new directory for the book and have subdirectories under that to organize the code chapter-wise. I have done this while writing this book. In the home directory of the `pi` user, that is `/home/pi`, I have created a directory book, which has three subdirectories: `code`, `test_set`, and `output`. The `code` subdirectory contains chapter-wise subdirectories which have code. The `test_set` directory contains all the test images we will use in our programs, and the output directory will be used to save images and videos as output of a few programs. The directory structure diagram is as follows:

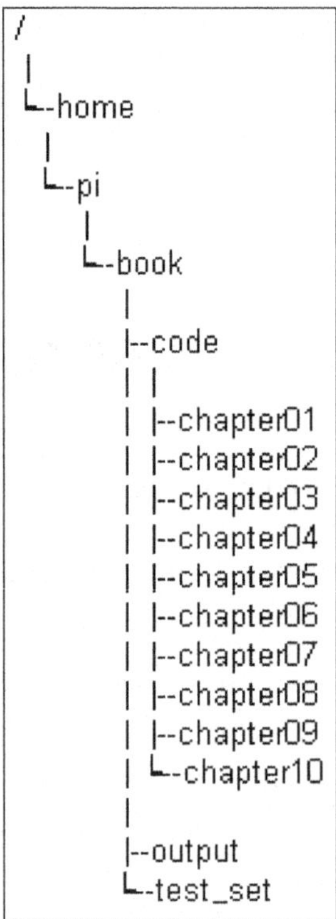

We will use images from http://sipi.usc.edu/database/ and http://www.imageprocessingplace.com/root_files_V3/image_databases.htm. These are standard test images used for image processing and computer vision.

Download the images (those that are in a compressed format) using your browser and unzip them in the test_set directory. Alternatively, you can directly download the compressed images to the test_set directory using the curl or wget utility and then unzip those.

Use the nano editor in LXTerminal to edit files. If you type nano prog1.py, nano will open prog1.py for editing if it already exists in the current directory; otherwise it will create a new file with the name prog1.py.

You can find more information about nano at http://www.nano-editor.org/.

Alternatively, you can use the Leafpad text editor. You can find it under **Accessories** in **Menu**. Or you can invoke it from command prompt with the following command:

```
leafpad prog1.py
```

Finally, you can also use vim, but you will need to install it by running the following command:

```
sudo apt-get install vim
```

For an interactive tutorial on **vim**, visit http://www.openvim.com/.

Let's write the same Python code and run it as a script. Write the following code with nano, leafpad, or vim and save it as test.py:

```
import cv2
print cv2.__version__
```

To run the preceding script, type python test.py in the editor. You should see the following output:

```
2.4.1
```

This is the version of OpenCV currently installed on your Pi.

Working with images

Let's get started with the basics of OpenCV's Python API. All the scripts we will write and run will be done using the OpenCV library, which must be imported with the line `import cv2`. We will import a few more libraries as needed in the next sections and chapters.

The `cv2.imread()` method is used to import an image. It takes two arguments. The first argument is the image filename. The image should either be in the same directory where the Python script is, or the absolute path should be provided to `cv2.imread()`. It reads images and saves it as a NumPy array.

The second argument is a flag which specifies the mode the image should be read in. The flag can have following values:

- `cv2.IMREAD_COLOR`: This loads a color image. This is the default flag.
- `cv2.IMREAD_GRAYSCALE`: This loads an image in grayscale mode.
- `cv2.IMREAD_UNCHANGED` : This loads an image as it is, including the alpha channel.

The numerical values of the preceding flags are 1, 0, and -1 respectively.

Take a look at the following code:

```
import cv2 #This imports opencv
#This reads and stores image in color into variable img
img = cv2.imread('/home/pi/book/test_set/
  lena_color_512.tif',cv2.IMREAD_COLOR)
```

Now, the last line in the preceding code is the same as the following:

```
img = cv2.imread('/home/pi/book/test_set/lena_color_512.tif',1)
```

We will be using the numeric values of this flag throughout the book.

The following code is used to display an image:

```
cv2.imshow('Lena',img)
cv2.waitKey(0)
cv2.destroyWindow('Lena')
```

The `cv2.imshow()` function is used to display an image. The first argument is a string, which is the window name, and the second argument is the variable that holds the image which is to be displayed.

The `cv2.waitKey()` function is a keyboard function. Its argument is the time in milliseconds. The function waits for specified milliseconds for any keyboard key press. If `0` is passed, it waits indefinitely for a key press. It is the only method to fetch and handle events. We must use this for using `cv2.imshow()` or no image will be displayed on screen.

The `cv2.destroyWindow()` function takes a window name as a parameter and destroys that window. If we want to destroy all the windows in the current program, we can use `cv2.destoyAllWindows()`.

We can also create a window with a specific name in advance and assign an image to that window later. In many cases, we will have to create a window before we have an image. This can be done using the following code:

```
cv2.namedWindow('Lena', cv2.WINDOW_AUTOSIZE)
cv2.imshow('Lena',img)
cv2.waitKey(0)
cv2.destroyAllWindows()
```

Putting it all together, we have the following script:

```
import cv2
img = cv2.imread('/home/pi/book/test_set/lena_color_512.tif',1)
cv2.imshow('Lena',img)
cv2.waitKey(0)
cv2.destroyWindow('Lena')
```

In summary, the preceding script imports an image, displays it, and waits for a keystroke to close the window. The screenshot is as follows:

The `cv2.imwrite()` method is used to save an image to a specific path. The first argument is the name of the file and the second is the variable pointing to the image we want to save. Also, `cv2.waitKey()` can be used to detect specific keystrokes. Let's test the usage of both the functions in the following code snippet:

```
import cv2
img = cv2.imread('/home/pi/book/test_set/lena_color_512.tif',1)
cv2.imshow('Lena',img)
keyPress = cv2.waitKey(0)
if keyPress == ord('q'):
cv2.destroyWindow('Lena')
elif keyPress == ord('s'): cv2.imwrite('/home/pi/book/
  output/chapter2_prog2_output.jpg',img)
  cv2.destroyWindow('Lena')
```

Here, `keyPress = cv2.waitKey(0)` is used to save the value of the keystroke in the `keyPress` variable. Given a string of length one, `ord()` returns an integer representing the Unicode code point of the character when the argument is a Unicode object, or the value of the byte when the argument is an 8-bit string. Based on `keyPress`, we are either exiting or exiting after saving an image. For example, if the *Esc* key is pressed, the `cv2.waitKey()` function would return 27.

Using matplotlib

We can also use matplotlib to display images. It is a 2D plotting library for Python. It provides a wide range of plotting options which we will be using in later chapters. Let's see a basic example of matplotlib:

```
import cv2
import matplotlib.pyplot as plt
# Program to load a color image in gray scale
  and to display using matplotlib
img = cv2.imread('/home/pi/book/test_set/lena_color_512.tif',0)
plt.imshow(img,cmap='gray')
plt.title('Lena')
plt.xticks([])
plt.yticks([])
plt.show()
```

Downloading the example code

You can download the example code files from your account at `http://www.packtpub.com` for all the Packt Publishing books you have purchased. If you purchased this book elsewhere, you can visit `http://www.packtpub.com/support` and register to have the files e-mailed directly to you.

In this example, we are reading an image in grayscale and displaying it using matplotlib. The following screenshot shows the plot of the image:

The `plt.xticks([])` and `plt.yticks([])` functions can be used to disable the *x* and *y* axis. Run the preceding code again, and this time, comment out the two lines with `plt.xticks([])` and `plt.yticks([])`.

The `cv2.imread()` function of OpenCV reads images and saves it as a NumPy array of **Blue, Green, and Red** (**BGR**) pixels.

However, `plt.imshow()` displays images in RGB format. So, if we read the image as it is with `cv2.imread()` and display it using `plt.imshow()`, the value of the Blue color will be treated as the value of Red and vice versa by `plt.imshow()`, and it would display the image with distorted colors. Try the preceding code with the following alterations in the respective lines to experience the concept:

```
img = cv2.imread('/home/pi/book/test_set/lena_color_512.tif',1)
plt.imshow(img)
```

To remedy this issue, we need to convert the image read in the BGR format into an RGB array format by `cv2.imread()` so that `plt.imshow()` will be able to render it in a way that makes sense to us. We will use the `cv2.cvtColor()` function for this, which will be introduced in *Chapter 3, Basic Image Processing*.

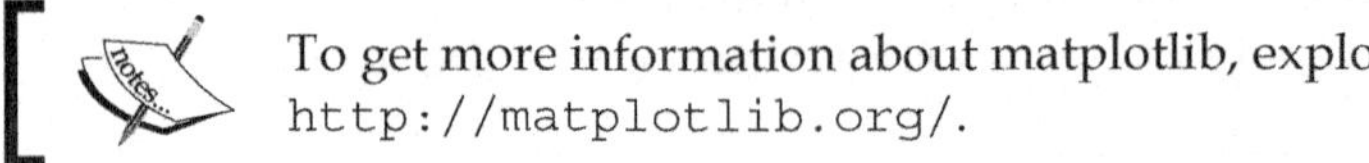

To get more information about matplotlib, explore http://matplotlib.org/.

Drawing geometric shapes

Let's get some hands on geometric shapes using OpenCV drawing functions. We are going to use NumPy here.

Import the necessary libraries with the following lines:

```
import cv2
import numpy as np
```

The following code creates a three-dimensional array of zeros, which is a black image with dimensions 200 x 200, as (0,0,0) represents the color black:

```
image = np.zeros((200,200,3), np.uint8)
```

The `np.zeros()` method makes an array with all elements equal to zero.

Now we will begin with a simple geometric shape that is a line. The following code draws a line with coordinates (0,199) and (199,0) in red color [(0,0,255) for BGR] with a thickness of 2:

```
cv2.line(image,(0,199),(199,0),(0,0,255),2)
```

Most of the OpenCV geometric functions have following common parameters:

- `img`: This refers to the image on which we need to draw shapes.
- `color`: This is passed as (B,G,R) where the value of each color ranges from 0 to 255.

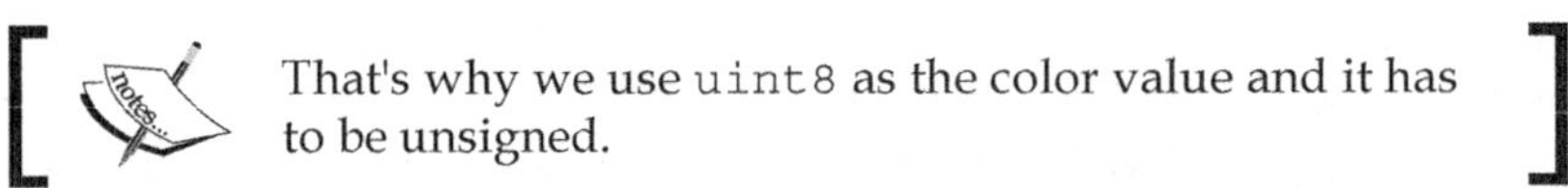

That's why we use `uint8` as the color value and it has to be unsigned.

- `thickness`: The default value is `1`. For all closed shapes such as a circle, ellipse and rectangle, `-1` will fill the shape with a specified color in that drawing function.

- `LineType`: It can have any one of following three values:
    - `8`: Eight connected lines (default value)
    - `4`: Four connected lines
    - `cv2.LINE_AA`: Anti-aliasing (great option for geometric shapes with curves, such as a circle and ellipse)

The following code draws a blue rectangle with (20,20) and (60,60) as diagonally opposite vertices:

```
cv2.rectangle(image,(20,20),(60,60),(255,0,0),1)
```

The following code draws a green filled circle with (80,80) as center and 10 as radius:

```
cv2.circle(image,(80,80),10,(0,255,0),-1)
```

The following code draws a full ellipse without any rotation with a center at (99,99) and major and minor axis lengths of 40 and 20 respectively:

```
cv2.ellipse(image,(99,99),(40,20),0,0,360,(128,128,128),-1)
```

The following code draws a polygon with four points:

```
points = np.array([[100,5],[125,30],[175,20],[185,10]], np.int32)
points = points.reshape((-1,1,2))
cv2.polylines(image,[points],True,(255,255,0))
```

If you pass `False` as the third argument in the `polylines()` function, it would join all the points and would not print a closed shape.

We can also print text in the image with `cv2.putText()`. The following code adds text to the image with (80,180) as the bottom-left corner of the text and `HERSHEY_DUPLEX` as the font with the size of 1 and color pink:

```
cv2.putText(image,'Test',(80,180), cv2.FONT_HERSHEY_DUPLEX ,
  1, (255,0,255))
```

The `cv2.putText()` function supports the following fonts:

- `FONT_HERSHEY_SIMPLEX`
- `FONT_HERSHEY_PLAIN`
- `FONT_HERSHEY_DUPLEX`

- `FONT_HERSHEY_COMPLEX`
- `FONT_HERSHEY_TRIPLEX`
- `FONT_HERSHEY_COMPLEX_SMALL`
- `FONT_HERSHEY_SCRIPT_SIMPLEX`
- `FONT_HERSHEY_SCRIPT_COMPLEX`

The final image is shown with our usual piece of code:

```
cv2.imshow('Shapes',image)
cv2.waitKey(0)
cv2.destroyAllWindows()
```

The output will be as follows:

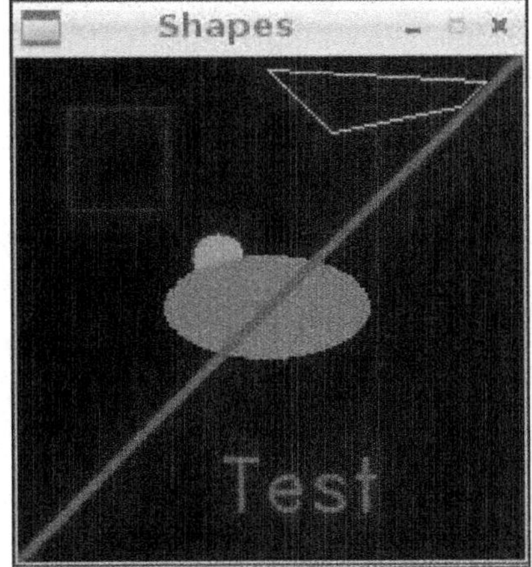

Note that the overlapping pixels are overwritten with values assigned by the most recent geometric function.

Now, try meddling with the values passed to all the functions and study the changes in output.

Working with trackbar and named window

In an earlier part of this book, we discussed the explicit creation of named window using `cv2.namedWindow()`. We will also see how to create a trackbar using `cv2.CreateTrackbar()` and how to use those to create a color palette for our use.

Take a look at the following code:

```
import numpy as np
import cv2

def empty(z):
    pass

# Create a black background
image = np.zeros((300,512,3), np.uint8)
cv2.namedWindow('Palette')

# create trackbars for colors and associate those with Pallete
cv2.createTrackbar('B','Palette',0,255,empty)
cv2.createTrackbar('G','Palette',0,255,empty)
cv2.createTrackbar('R','Palette',0,255,empty)

while(True):
    cv2.imshow('Palette',image)
    if cv2.waitKey(1) == 27:
        break

    # fetch the color value
    blue = cv2.getTrackbarPos('B','Palette')
    green = cv2.getTrackbarPos('G','Palette')
    red = cv2.getTrackbarPos('R','Palette')

    image[:] = [blue,green,red]

cv2.destroyWindow('Pallete')
```

In the preceding code, we are first creating a black background and a named window with the name `Palette`. The `cv2.createTrackbar()` method creates a trackbar and takes the following parameters:

- `Name`: This refers to the name of the trackbar to be created.
- `Window_name`: This specifies the name of the named window to be associated with.
- `Value`: This refers to the initial value of the slider when created.
- `Count`: This is the maximum value of the slider—the minimum is always 0.
- `Onchange()`: This function is called when the slider changes position.

We have created an `empty()` function as we are not performing any activity when the slider is changed, and we're passing this function to `cv2.createTrackbar()`. The `cv2.getTrackbarPos()` function returns the current position of the specified trackbar. We check the position of the trackbars and create a color palette based on the positions selected repeatedly until a key is pressed, ending the infinite loop and stopping the program.

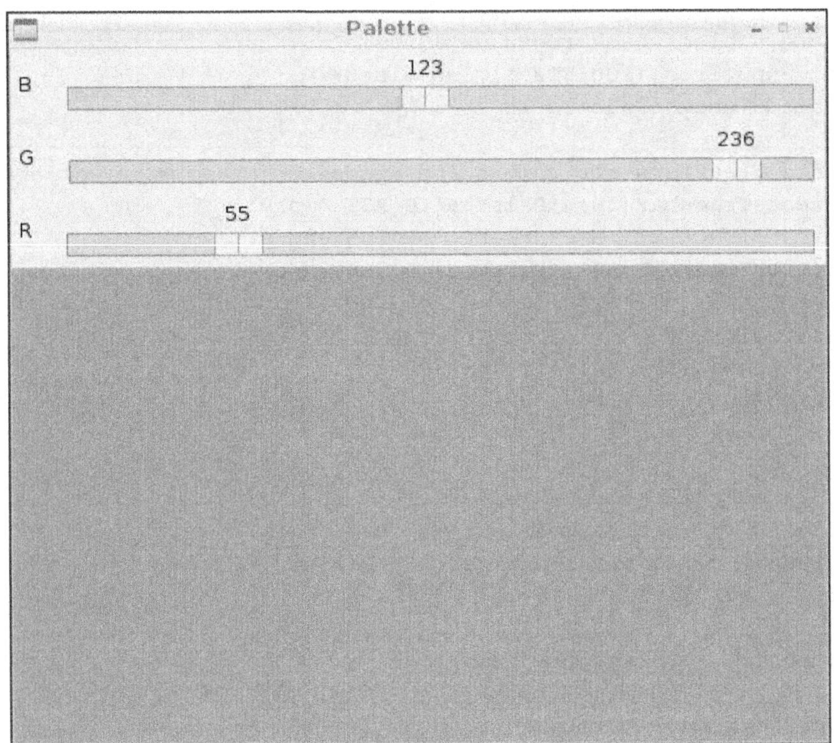

Working with a webcam

USB webcams are great to capture images and videos. Raspberry Pi supports most USB webcams.

> To be on the safe side, go through the list of supported webcams by Pi at `http://elinux.org/RPi_USB_Webcams`.

I am using a Logitech HD c310 USB webcam.

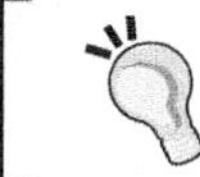

> You can purchase this webcam from Amazon, and you can find the product details at `http://www.logitech.com/en-in/product/hd-webcam-c310`.

Attach your USB webcam to Raspberry Pi through the USB port on Pi and run the `lsusb` command in the terminal. This command lists all the USB devices connected to the computer. The output should be similar to the following output, depending on which port is used to connect the USB webcam:

```
pi@pi02 ~/book/code/chapter02 $ lsusb
Bus 001 Device 002: ID 0424:9514 Standard Microsystems Corp.
Bus 001 Device 001: ID 1d6b:0002 Linux Foundation 2.0 root hub
Bus 001 Device 003: ID 0424:ec00 Standard Microsystems Corp.
Bus 001 Device 007: ID 046d:081b Logitech, Inc. Webcam C310
Bus 001 Device 016: ID 1a2c:0c21
Bus 001 Device 006: ID 1c4f:0003 SiGma Micro HID controller
```

Then, install the `fswebcam` utility with the `sudo apt-get install fswebcam` command. Once the installation is done, you can use the following command to capture the image:

```
fswebcam -r 1280x960 --no-banner ~/book/output/camtest.jpg
```

This will capture an image with a resolution of 1280 x 960. The `--no-banner` parameter will disable the timestamp banner, and the image will be saved with the filename mentioned. If you run this command multiple times with the same filename, each time the image file will be overwritten. So, make sure that you change the filename if you want to save earlier captured images. The output of the command should be similar to the following:

```
--- Opening /dev/video0...
Trying source module v4l2...
/dev/video0 opened.
No input was specified, using the first.
--- Capturing frame...
Corrupt JPEG data: 1 extraneous bytes before marker 0xd0
Captured frame in 0.00 seconds.
--- Processing captured image...
Disabling banner.
Writing JPEG image to '/home/pi/book/output/camtest.jpg'.
```

Creating a timelapse sequence using fswebcam

Timelapse photography means capturing photographs at a regular interval and playing those images at a higher frequency than in the time they were shot. For example, if you captured images with a frequency of 1 image per minute for 10 hours, you would get 600 images. If you combined all those images in a video with 30 images per second, you would get 10 hours of timelapse, compressed in 20 seconds. You can use your USB webcam with Raspberry Pi to achieve this. We already know how to use Raspberry Pi with a webcam and the `fswebcam` utility to capture an image. The trick is to write a script which captures images with different names and then to add this script in `crontab` to run at regular intervals. Cron is a time-based job scheduler in Unix-like computer operating systems. It is driven by a **crontab (cron table)** file, a configuration file that specifies shell commands to run periodically on a given schedule.

Open an editor of your choice and write the following code and save it as `timelapse.sh`:

```
#!/bin/bash

DATE=$(date +"%Y-%m-%d_%H%M")

fswebcam -r 1280x960 --no-banner
/home/pi/book/output/timelapse/garden_$DATE.jpg
```

Make the script executable using `chmod +x timelapse.sh`.

This shell script captures the image and saves it with the current timestamp in its name. Thus, we get an image with a new filename every time. Run this script manually once and make sure that the image is saved in the `/home/pi/book/output/timelapse` directory with the name `garden_<timestamp>.jpg`.

To run this script at regular intervals, we need to schedule it in `crontab`. Easy-to-remember `crontab` syntax is as follows:

```
1 2 3 4 5 /location/command
```

In this syntax:

- `1`: Minute (0-59)
- `2`: Hours (0-23)
- `3`: Day (0-31)

- `4`: Month (0-12 [1 for January])
- `5`: Day of the week (0-7 [7 or 0 for Sunday])
- `/location/command`: Script or command name to schedule

So, the `crontab` entry to run the script every minute is as follows:

```
* * * * * /home/pi/book/code/chapter02/timelapse.sh 2>&1
```

Open `crontab` of the Pi user with `crontab -e`. It will open `crontab` with `nano` as editor. Add the preceding line to `crontab` and save and exit it.

Once you exit `crontab`, it will show following message:

```
crontab: installing new crontab
```

Our timelapse webcam setup is live. If you want to change the image capture frequency, you have to change the `crontab` settings. To set it for every 5 minutes, change it to `*/5 * * * *`. To set it for every 2 hours, use `0 */2 * * *`. Make sure that your microSD card has enough free space to store all the images for the time duration you need to keep your timelapse setup.

Once you capture all the images, the next part is to encode them all in a fast-playing video, preferably 20 to 30 frames per second. Raspberry Pi is a slow machine to do all this encoding. It is recommended to transfer the images to a faster machine for encoding. For Linux machines, the MEncoder utility is recommended. Following are the steps required to create a timelapse video with MEncoder on Raspberry Pi or any Debian machine:

1. Install MEncoder using `sudo apt-get install mencoder`.
2. Navigate to the output directory by issuing `cd /home/pi/book/output/timelapse`.
3. Create a list of your timelapse sequence images using `ls garden_*.jpg > timelapse.txt`.
4. Finally, use the following command to create a video:

```
mencoder -nosound -ovc lavc -lavcopts
  vcodec=mpeg4:aspect=16/9:vbitrate=8000000 -vf
  scale=1280:960 -o timelapse.avi -mf type=jpeg:fps=30
  mf://@timelapse.txt
```

This will create a video with the name `timelapse.avi` in the current directory with all the images listed in `timelapse.txt` with 30 fps framerate. We will see how to play a video shortly.

Webcam video recording and playback

We can use the webcam to record live videos using **avconv**. Install avconv using `sudo apt-get install avconv`. Use the following command to record a video—you can terminate the recording sequence by pressing *Ctrl* + *C*:

```
avconv -f video4linux2 -r 25 -s 544x288 -i /dev/video0
  ~/book/output/VideoStream.avi
```

We can play the video using omxplayer. It comes with latest Raspbian, so there is no need to install it. To play a file with the name `vid.mjpg`, use the following command:

```
omxplayer vid.mjpg
```

It will show output similar to the following:

```
Video codec omx-h264 width 1920 height 1080 profile 100 fps
  25.000000
Subtitle count: 0, state: off, index: 1, delay: 0
V:PortSettingsChanged: 1920x1080@25.00 interlace:0 deinterlace:0
  anaglyph:0 par:1.00 layer:0
have a nice day ;)
```

Try playing timelapse and recorded videos using omxplayer.

Working with a webcam using OpenCV

OpenCV has a functionality to work with standard USB webcams. Let's see an example of capturing an image from a webcam using OpenCV:

```
import cv2

# initialize the camera
cam = cv2.VideoCapture(0)
ret, image = cam.read()

if ret:
    cv2.imshow('SnapshotTest',image)
    cv2.waitKey(0)
    cv2.destroyWindow('SnapshotTest')
    cv2.imwrite('/home/pi/book/output/SnapshotTest.jpg',image)
cam.release()
```

In the preceding code, `cv2.VideoCapture()` creates a video capture object. The argument for it could either be a video device or a file. In this case, we are passing the device index which is `0`. If we have more cameras, we can pass the appropriate device index based on what camera to choose. If you have one camera, just pass `0`.

You can find out the number of cameras and associated device indexes by using the `ls -l /dev/video*` command.

Once `cam.read()` returns a Boolean value `ret` and the frame, which is the image it captured. If the image capture is successful, then return will be `True`; otherwise, it will be `false`. The preceding code captures an image with the camera device `/dev/video0`, displays it and then saves it. The `cam.release()` method releases the device.

The same code could be used with slight modifications to display a live video stream from a webcam:

```
import cv2

cam = cv2.VideoCapture(0)
print 'Default Resolution is ' + str(int(cam.get(3))) + 'x' +
  str(int(cam.get(4)))
w=1024
h=768
cam.set(3,w)
cam.set(4,h)
print 'Now resolution is set to ' + str(w) + 'x' + str(h)

while(True):
    # Capture frame-by-frame
    ret, frame = cam.read()

    # Display the resulting frame
    cv2.imshow('Video Test',frame)

    # Wait for Escape Key
    if cv2.waitKey(1) == 27 :
        break

# When everything done, release the capture
cam.release()
cv2.destroyAllWindows()
```

You can access the features of the video device with `cam.get(propertyID)`. `3` stands for width and `4` stands for height. These properties could be set with `cam.set(propertyID, value)`.

The preceding code first displays the default resolution and then sets it to 1024 x 768, displaying the live video stream until the *Esc* key is pressed. This is the basic skeleton logic for all live video processing with OpenCV. We will make use of this regularly throughout this book.

Saving a video and playback of a video using OpenCV

We use the `cv2.VideoWriter()` function to write a video to a file. Take a look at following code:

```
import cv2

cam = cv2.VideoCapture(0)

output  = cv2.VideoWriter('/home/pi/book/output/
  VideoStream.avi',cv2.cv.CV_FOURCC(*'WMV2'),40.0,(640,480))

while (cam.isOpened()):
  ret, frame = cam.read()
  if ret == True:
    output.write(frame)
    cv2.imshow('VideoStream', frame )
    if cv2.waitKey(1) == 27 :
      break
  else:
    break

cam.release()
output.release()
cv2.destroyAllWindows()
```

In the preceding code, `cv2.VideoWriter()` accepts the following parameters:

- Filename: This refers to the name of the video file.
- FourCC: This stands for Four Character Code. We use the `cv2.cv.CV_FOURCC()` function for this. This function accepts FourCC in `*'code'` format. This means for DIVX, we need to pass `*'DIVX'` and so on. A few supported formats are DIVX, XVID, H264, MJPG, WMV1, and WMV2. You can read more about FourCC at `www.fourcc.org`.

- Framerate: This refers to the rate of frames to be captured per second.
- Resolution: This specifies the resolution of the video to be captured.

The preceding code records the video until the *Esc* key is pressed and saves it in the specified file.

Working with the Pi camera module

This camera module is specially manufactured for Raspberry Pi and works with all the available models. You will need to connect the camera module to the CSI port, located behind the Ethernet port, and activate the camera using the `raspi-config` utility.

> You can find video instructions to connect the camera module to Raspberry Pi at `http://www.raspberrypi.org/help/camera-module-setup/`.
>
> The types of camera modules available are listed at `http://www.raspberrypi.org/products/`.

Using raspistill and raspivid

To capture images and videos using the Raspberry Pi camera module, we need to use the `raspistill` and `raspivid` utilities.

To capture an image, run following command:

```
raspistill -o cam_module_pic.jpg
```

This will capture and save the image with the name `cam_module_pic.jpg`.

To capture a 20-second video with the camera module, run the following command:

```
Raspivid -o test.avi -t 20000
```

Unlike `fswebcam` and `avconv`, `raspistill` and `raspivid` do not write anything to the console. So you need to check the current directory for the output. Also, one can run the `echo $?` command to check if these commands have been executed successfully.

Just like `fswebcam`, `raspistill` can be used to record a timelapse sequence. In our timelapse shell script, replace the line which contains `fswebcam` with the appropriate `raspistill` command to capture a timelapse sequence and use MEncoder again to create the video.

Using picamera in Python with the Pi camera module

picamera is a python package which provides a programming interface to the Pi camera module. The most recent version of Raspbian has picamera installed. If you do not have it installed, you can install it using `sudo apt-get install python-picamera`.

The following program quickly demonstrates the basic usage of the picamera module to capture a picture:

```
import picamera
import time

with picamera.PiCamera() as cam:
  cam.resolution=(1024,768)
  cam.start_preview()
  time.sleep(5)
  cam.capture('/home/pi/book/output/still.jpg')
```

We have to import time and picamera modules first. The `cam.start_preview()` method starts the preview and `time.sleep(5)` waits for 5 seconds before `cam.capture()` captures and saves the image in the specified file.

There is an inbuilt function in picamera for timelapse photography. Let's see its usage using the following program:

```
import picamera
import time

with picamera.PiCamera() as cam:
  cam.resolution=(640,480)
  cam.start_preview()
  time.sleep(3)
  for count, imagefile in enumerate(cam.capture_continuous(
    '/home/pi/book/output/image{counter:02d}.jpg')):
    print 'Capturing and saving ' + imagefile
    time.sleep(1)
    if count == 10:
      break
```

In the preceding code, `cam.capture_continuous()` is used to capture the timelapse sequence using the Pi camera module.

Find more examples and API reference for the Pi camera module at `http://picamera.readthedocs.org/`.

picamera and OpenCV

The following code demonstrates the use of picamera with OpenCV; it shows a preview for 3 seconds, captures an image, and displays it on screen using `cv2.imshow()`:

```
import picamera
import picamera.array
import time
import cv2

with picamera.PiCamera() as camera:
  rawCap=picamera.array.PiRGBArray(camera)
  camera.start_preview()
  time.sleep(3)
  camera.capture(rawCap,format="bgr")
  image=rawCap.array
cv2.imshow("Test",image)
cv2.waitKey(0)
cv2.destroyAllWindows()
```

Summary

In this chapter, we explored how to work with images and videos, and how to implement basic GUIs. We also saw how to use a webcam in OpenCV and how to use a webcam and picamera for timelapse setup. We will be reusing all the code examples we studied in this chapter throughout the book.

In the next chapter, we will get our hands on basic image processing operations, such as mathematical and logical operators on images. We will also take a look at topics such as splitting an image color channel and inverting an image.

3
Basic Image Processing

In the previous chapter, we learned how to work with images and videos, create a basic GUI, and use cameras to capture images and videos. In this chapter, we will study the basic image processing in OpenCV. We will do this with the help of the following topics:

- Retrieving the properties of an image
- Image arithmetic operations—adding, subtracting, and blending images
- Splitting color channels in an image
- Negating an image
- Performing logical operations on an image

This chapter is very short and easy to code with plenty of hands-on activities.

Retrieving image properties

We can retrieve and use many properties of an image with OpenCV functions. Have a look at the following code:

```
import cv2
img = cv2.imread('/home/pi/book/test_set/lena_color_512.tif',1)
print img.shape
print img.size
print img.dtype
```

The `img.shape` function returns the shape of an image, that is, its dimensions and the number of color channels. The output of the preceding code is as follows:

```
pi@pi02 ~/book/code/chapter03 $ python prog1.py
(512, 512, 3)
786432
uint8
```

If the image is colored, then `img.shape` returns a triplet containing the number of rows, columns, and channels in the image. Usually, the number of channels is three, representing the red, green, and blue channels. If the image is grayscale, then `img.shape` only returns the number of rows and columns. Try modifying the preceding code to read the image in grayscale mode and observe the output of `img.shape`.

The `img.size` function returns the total number of pixels and `img.dtype` returns the image data type.

Arithmetic operations on images

In this section, we will have a look at the various arithmetic operations that can be performed on images. Images are represented as matrices in OpenCV. So, arithmetic operations on images are similar to the arithmetic operations on matrices. Images must be of the same size for you to perform arithmetic operations on the images, and these operations are performed on individual pixels.

- `cv2.add()`: This function is used to add two images, where the images are passed as parameters.
- `cv2.subtract()`: This function is used to subtract an image from another.

We know that the subtraction operation is not commutative. So, `cv2.subtract(img1,img2)` and `cv2.(img2,img1)` will yield different results, whereas `cv2.add(img1,img2)` and `cv2.add(img2,img1)` will yield the same result as the addition operation is commutative. Both the images have to be of same size and type, as explained before.

Check out the following code:

```
import cv2
img1 = cv2.imread('/home/pi/book/test_set/4.2.03.tiff',1)
img2 = cv2.imread('/home/pi/book/test_set/4.2.04.tiff',1)
cv2.imshow('Image1',img1)
cv2.waitKey(0)
cv2.imshow('Image2',img2)
cv2.waitKey(0)
cv2.imshow('Addition',cv2.add(img1,img2))
cv2.waitKey(0)
cv2.imshow('Image1-Image2',cv2.subtract(img1,img2))
cv2.waitKey(0)
cv2.imshow('Image2-Image1',cv2.subtract(img2,img1))
cv2.waitKey(0)
cv2.destroyAllWindows()
```

The preceding code demonstrates the usage of arithmetic functions on images. Image 2 is the same Lena image that we experimented with in the previous chapter. So I am not going to include its output window. Here's the output window of Image1:

Here is the output window of **Addition**:

The output window of *Image1-Image2* looks like this:

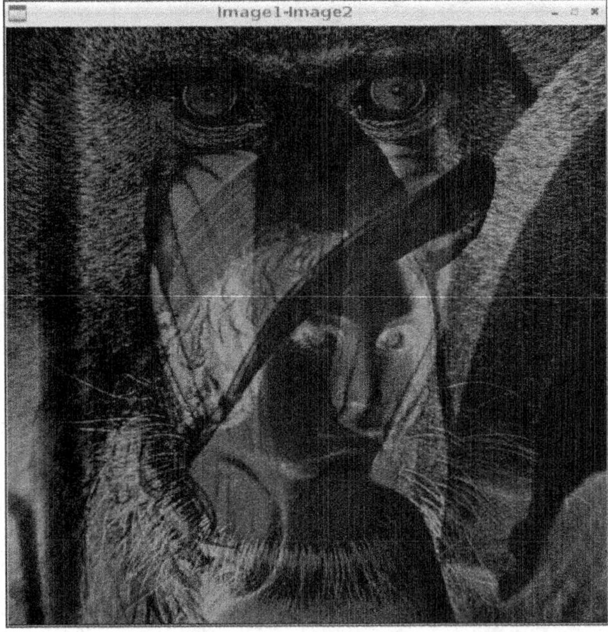

Here is the output window of *Image2-Image1*:

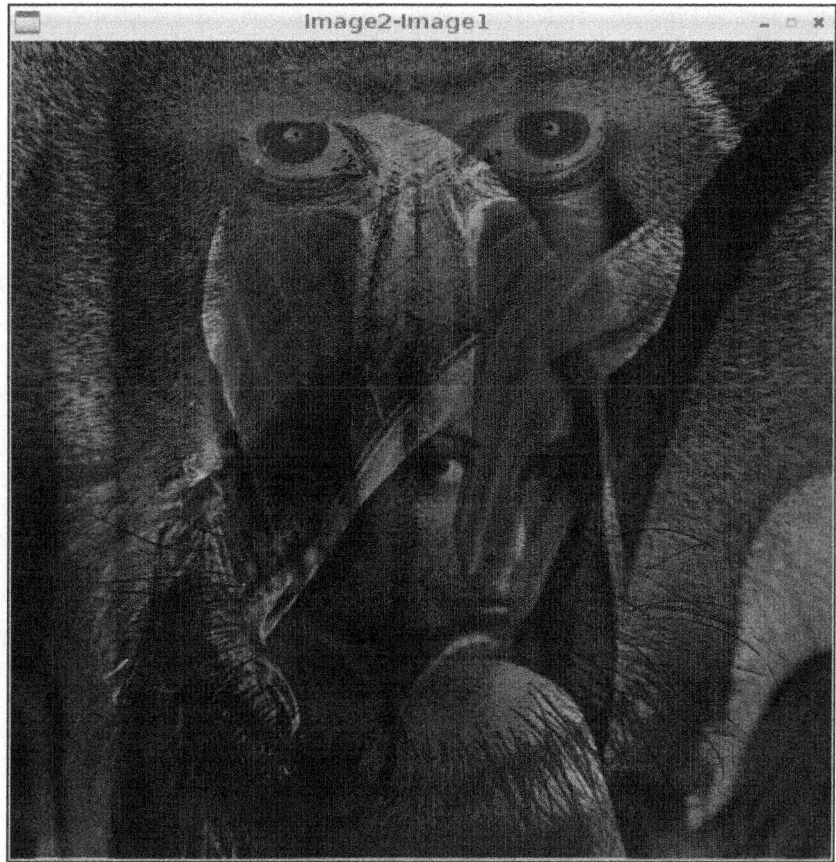

Blending and transitioning images

The `cv2.addWeighted()` function calculates the weighted sum of two images. Because of the weight factor, it provides a blending effect to the images. Add the following lines of code before `destroyAllWindows()` in the previous code listing to see this function in action:

```
cv2.addWeighted(img1,0.5,img2,0.5,0)
cv2.waitKey(0)
```

In the preceding code, we passed the following five arguments to the `addWeighted()` function:

- `Img1`: This is the first image.
- `Alpha`: This is the weight factor for the first image (0.5 in the example).
- `Img2`: This is the second image.
- `Beta`: This is the weight factor for the second image (0.5 in the example).
- `Gamma`: This is the scalar value (0 in the example).

The output image value is calculated with the following formula:

$$\text{Output} = (\text{alpha} * \text{img}1) + (\text{beta} * \text{img}2) + \text{gamma}$$

This operation is performed on every individual pixel.

Here is the output of the preceding code:

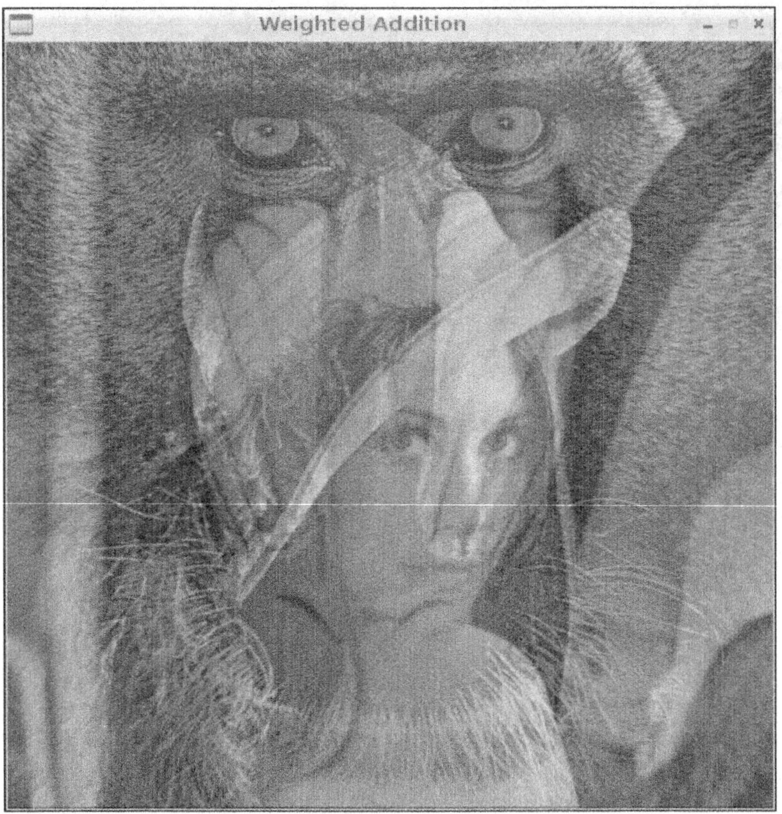

We can create a film-style transition effect on the two images by using the same function. Check out the output of the following code that creates a smooth image transition from an image to another image:

```
import cv2
import numpy as np
import time

img1 = cv2.imread('/home/pi/book/test_set/4.2.03.tiff',1)
img2 = cv2.imread('/home/pi/book/test_set/4.2.04.tiff',1)

for i in np.linspace(0,1,40):
  alpha=i
  beta=1-alpha
  print 'ALPHA ='+ str(alpha)+' BETA ='+str (beta)
  cv2.imshow('Image Transition',
    cv2.addWeighted(img1,alpha,img2,beta,0))
  time.sleep(0.05)
  if cv2.waitKey(1) == 27 :
    break

cv2.destroyAllWindows()
```

Splitting and merging image colour channels

On several occasions, we may be interested in working separately with the red, green, and blue channels. For example, we might want to build a histogram for every channel of an image.

We will work separately with the different channels in *Chapter 8, Histograms, Contours, Morphological Transformations, and Performance Measurement*.

Here, `cv2.split()` is used to split an image into three different intensity arrays for each color channel, whereas `cv2.merge()` is used to merge different arrays into a single multi-channel array, that is, a color image.

The following example demonstrates this:

```
import cv2
img = cv2.imread('/home/pi/book/test_set/4.2.03.tiff',1)
b,g,r = cv2.split (img)
cv2.imshow('Blue Channel',b)
cv2.imshow('Green Channel',g)
cv2.imshow('Red Channel',r)
img=cv2.merge((b,g,r))
cv2.imshow('Merged Output',img)
cv2.waitKey(0)
cv2.destroyAllWindows()
```

The preceding program first splits the image into three channels (blue, green, and red) and then displays each one of them. The separate channels will only hold the intensity values of the particular color and the images will essentially be displayed as grayscale intensity images. Then, the program merges all the channels back into an image and displays it.

Creating a negative of an image

In mathematical terms, the negative of an image is the inversion of colors. For a grayscale image, it is even simpler! The negative of a grayscale image is just the intensity inversion, which can be achieved by finding the complement of the intensity from 255. A pixel value ranges from 0 to 255, and therefore, negation involves the subtracting of the pixel value from the maximum value, that is, 255. The code for the same is as follows:

```
import cv2
img = cv2.imread('/home/pi/book/test_set/4.2.07.tiff')
grayscale = cv2.cvtColor(img,cv2.COLOR_BGR2GRAY)
negative = abs(255-grayscale)
cv2.imshow('Original',img)
cv2.imshow('Grayscale',grayscale)
cv2.imshow('Negative',negative)
cv2.waitKey(0)
cv2.destroyAllWindows()
```

Here is the output window of *Greyscale*:

Here's the output window of *Negative*:

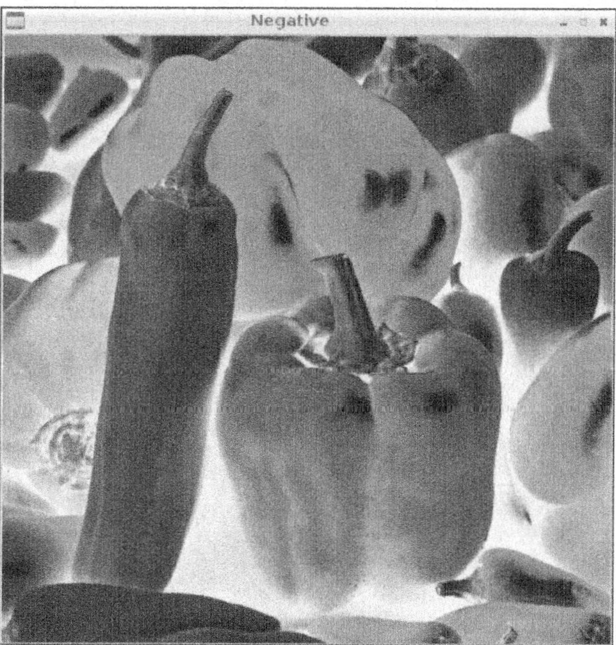

The negative of a negative will be the original grayscale image. Try this on your own by taking the image negative of the negative again.

Logical operations on images

OpenCV provides bitwise logical operation functions for images. We will have a look at the functions that provide the bitwise logical AND, OR, XOR (exclusive OR), and NOT (inversion) functionality. These functions can be better demonstrated visually with grayscale images. I am going to use barcode images in horizontal and vertical orientation for demonstration. Let's have a look at the following code:

```
import cv2
import matplotlib.pyplot as plt

img1 = cv2.imread('/home/pi/book/test_set/Barcode_Hor.png',0)
img2 = cv2.imread('/home/pi/book/test_set/Barcode_Ver.png',0)
not_out=cv2.bitwise_not(img1)
and_out=cv2.bitwise_and(img1,img2)
or_out=cv2.bitwise_or(img1,img2)
xor_out=cv2.bitwise_xor(img1,img2)

titles = ['Image 1','Image 2','Image 1 NOT','AND','OR','XOR']
images = [img1,img2,not_out,and_out,or_out,xor_out]

for i in xrange(6):
    plt.subplot(2,3,i+1)
    plt.imshow(images[i],cmap='gray')
    plt.title(titles[i])
    plt.xticks([]),plt.yticks([])
plt.show()
```

We first read the images in grayscale mode and calculated the NOT, AND, OR, and XOR, functionalities and then with matplotlib, we displayed those in a neat way. We leveraged the `plt.subplot()` function to display multiple images. Here in the preceding example, we created a grid with two rows and three columns for our images and displayed each image in every part of the grid. You can modify this line and change it to `plt.subplot(3,2,i+1)` to create a grid with three rows and two columns. We will use this technique heavily throughout the book to display images side-by-side or in a grid.

Also, we can use the technique without a loop in the following way. For each image, you have to write the following statements. I will write the code for the first image only. Go ahead and write it for the rest of the five images:

```
plt.subplot(2,3,1) , plt.imshow(img1,cmap='gray') ,
  plt.title('Image 1') , plt.xticks([]),plt.yticks([])
```

Finally, use `plt.show()` to display. This technique is to avoid the loop when a very small number of images, usually 2 or 3 in number, have to be displayed. The output of this is as follows:

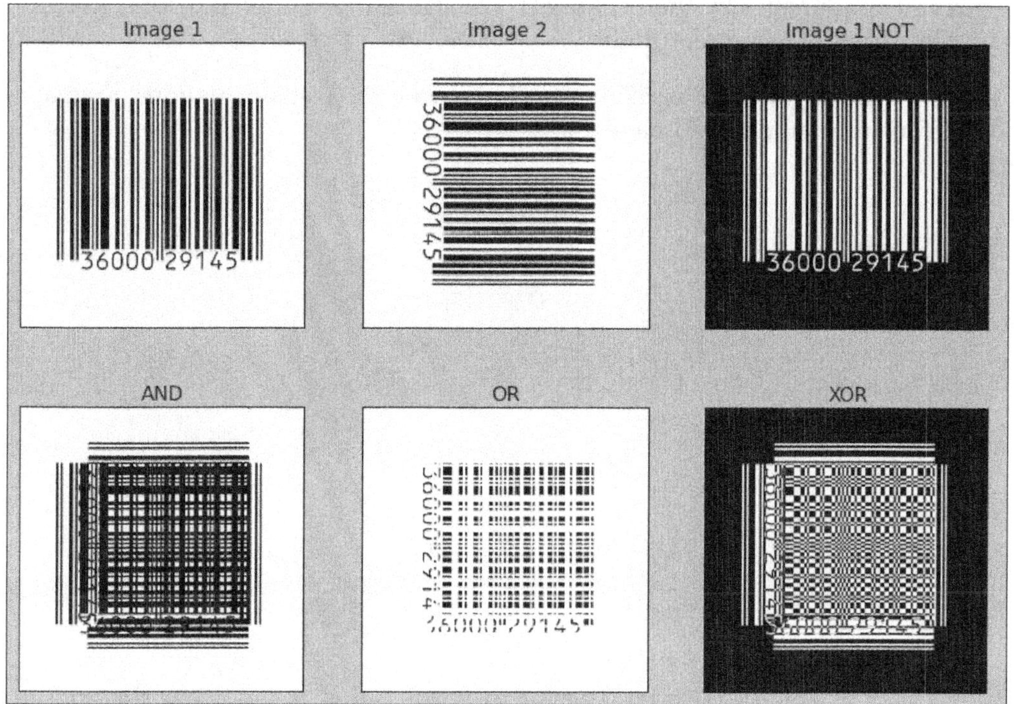

Make a note of the fact that the logical NOT operation is the negative of the image.

Exercise

You may want to have a look at the functionality of `cv2.copyMakeBorder()`. This function is used to create the borders and paddings for images, and many of you will find it useful for your projects. We won't use this function in the remainder of our book. So, the exploring of this function is left as an exercise for the readers.

You can check the python OpenCV API documentation at the following location:

http://docs.opencv.org/modules/refman.html

Summary

In this chapter, we learned how to perform arithmetic and logical operations on images and split images by their channels. We also learned how to display multiple images in a grid by using matplotlib.

In the next chapter, we will learn about color spaces, the transformations on images, and the various gradients of images.

4
Colorspaces, Transformations, and Thresholds

In our previous chapter, we saw how to perform basic mathematical and logical operations on images. We also saw how to use these operations to create a film-style smooth image transitioning effect. In this chapter, we will continue to explore a few more intriguing computer vision concepts and their applications in the real world. We will explore the following topics:

- Colorspaces and conversions
- Real-time object tracking based on color value
- Geometric transformations on images
- Thresholding an image

Colorspaces and conversions

A colorspace is a mathematical model used to represent colors. Usually, colorspaces are used to represent the colors in a numerical form and to perform mathematical and logical operations with them. In this book, the colorspaces we mostly use are BGR (OpenCV's default colorspace), RGB, HSV, and grayscale. **BGR** stands for **blue**, **green**, and **red**. **HSV** represents colors in **Hue**, **Saturation**, and **Value** format. OpenCV has a function `cv2.cvtColor(img,conv_flag)` that allows us to change the colorspace of an image (`img`), while the source and target colorspaces are indicated on the `conv_flag` parameter.

If you remember, in *Chapter 2, Working with Images, Webcams, and GUI*, we discovered that OpenCV loads images in BGR format and matplotlib uses the RGB format for images. So, before displaying an image with matplotlib, we need to convert an image from BGR to RGB colorspace.

Take a look at the following code. The program reads the image in color mode using `cv2.imread()`, which imports the image in the BGR colorspace. Then, it converts it to RGB using `cv2.cvtColor()`, and finally, it uses matplotlib to display the image:

```
import cv2
import matplotlib.pyplot as plt

img = cv2.imread('/home/pi/book/test_set/4.2.07.tiff',1)
img = cv2.cvtColor ( img , cv2.COLOR_BGR2RGB )
plt.imshow ( img ) , plt.title ('COLOR IMAGE'),
  plt.xticks([]) , plt.yticks([])
plt.show()
```

Another way to convert an image from BGR to RGB is to first split the image into three separate channels (B, G, and R channels) and merge them in BGR order. However, this takes more time as split and merge operations are inherently computationally costly, making them slower and inefficient. So, for the remainder of this book, we will use the first method. The following code shows this method:

```
import cv2
import matplotlib.pyplot as plt
img = cv2.imread('/home/pi/book/test_set/4.2.07.tiff',1)
b,g,r = cv2.split ( img )
img=cv2.merge((r,g,b))
plt.imshow ( img ) , plt.title ('COLOR IMAGE'), plt.xticks([]) , plt.
yticks([])
plt.show()
```

The output of both the programs is the same as shown in the following image:

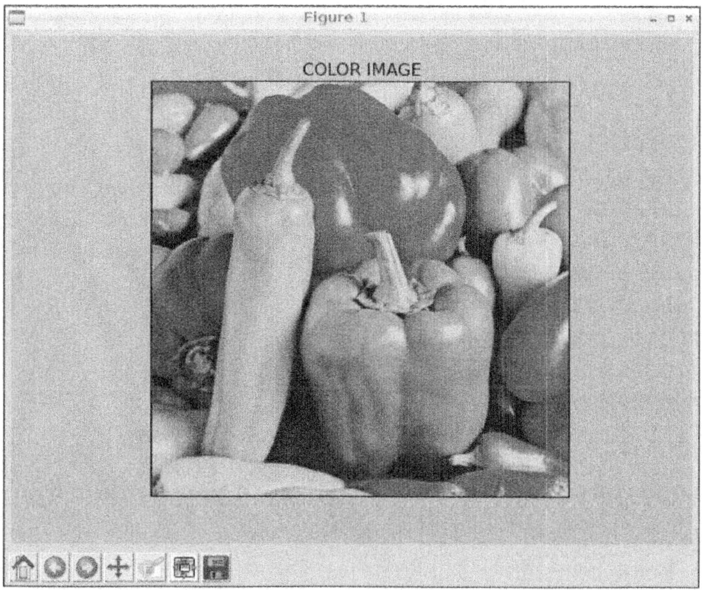

If you need to know the colorspace conversion flags, then the following snippet of code will assist you in finding the list of available flags for your current OpenCV installation:

```
import cv2
j=0
for filename in dir(cv2):
  if filename.startswith('COLOR_'):
    print filename
    j=j+1

print 'There are ' + str(j) + ' Colorspace Conversion
  flags in OpenCV'
```

The last few lines of the output will be as follows (I am not including the complete output due to space limitation):

```
.
.
.
COLOR_YUV420P2BGRA
COLOR_YUV420P2GRAY
COLOR_YUV420P2RGB
COLOR_YUV420P2RGBA
COLOR_YUV420SP2BGR
COLOR_YUV420SP2BGRA
COLOR_YUV420SP2GRAY
COLOR_YUV420SP2RGB
COLOR_YUV420SP2RGBA
There are 176 Colorspace Conversion flags in OpenCV
```

The following code converts a color from BGR to HSV and prints it:

```
>>> import cv2
>>> import numpy as np
>>> c =  cv2.cvtColor(np.uint8[[[255,0,0]]]),cv2.COLOR_BGR2HSV)
>>> print c
[[[120 255 255]]]
```

The preceding snippet of code prints the HSV value of the color blue represented in BGR.

Hue, Saturation, Value, or HSV is a color model that describes colors (hue or tint) in terms of their shade (saturation or amount of gray) and their brightness (value or luminance). Hue is expressed as a number representing hues of red, yellow, green, cyan, blue, and magenta. Saturation is the amount of gray in the color. Value works in conjunction with saturation and describes the brightness or intensity of the color.

Tracking in real time based on color

Let's study a real-life application of this concept. In HSV format, it's much easier to recognize the color range. If we need to track a specific color object, we will have to define a color range in HSV, then convert the captured image in the HSV format, and then check whether the part of that image falls within the HSV color range of our interest. We can use the `cv2.inRange()` function to achieve this. This function takes an image, the upper and lower bounds of the colors, and then checks the range criteria for each pixel. If the pixel value falls in the given color range, the corresponding pixel in the output image is 0; otherwise it is 255, thus creating a binary mask.

We can use `bitwise_and()` to extract the color range we're interested in using this binary mask thereafter. Take a look at the following code to understand this concept:

```
import numpy as np
import cv2

cam = cv2.VideoCapture(0)

while ( True ):
        ret, frame = cam.read()

        hsv=cv2.cvtColor(frame,cv2.COLOR_BGR2HSV)

        image_mask=cv2.inRange(hsv,np.array([40,50,50]),
          np.array([80,255,255]))

        output=cv2.bitwise_and(frame,frame,mask=image_mask)

        cv2.imshow('Original',frame)
        cv2.imshow('Output',output)

        if cv2.waitKey(1) == 27:
                break

cv2.destroyAllWindows()
cam.release()
```

We're tracking the green colored objects in this program. The output should be similar to the following one. I used green tea bag tags as the test object.

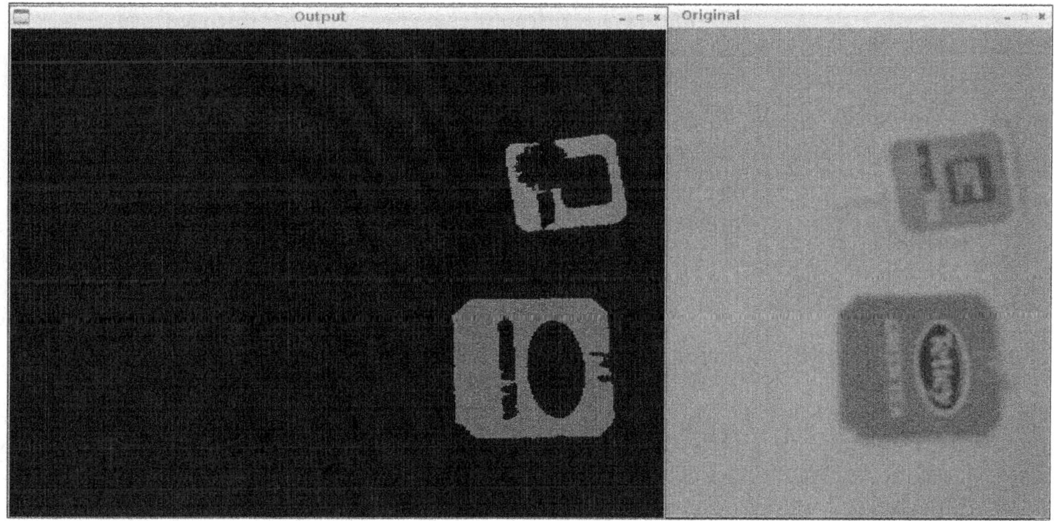

The mask image is not included in the preceding image. You can see it yourself by adding `cv2.imshow('Image Mask',image_mask)` to the code. It would be a binary (pure black and white) image.

We can also track multiple colors by tweaking this code a bit. We need to modify the preceding code by creating a mask for another color range. Then, we can use `cv2.add()` to get the combined mask for two distinct color ranges, as follows:

```
blue=cv2.inRange(hsv,np.array([100,50,50]),np.array([140,255,255]))
green=cv2.inRange(hsv,np.array([40,50,50]),np.array([80,255,255]))
image_mask=cv2.add(blue,green)
output=cv2.bitwise_and(frame,frame,mask=image_mask)
```

Try this code and check the output for yourself.

Image transformations

In this section, we will see the various transformations on an image, and how to implement them in OpenCV.

Scaling

Scaling is the resizing of the image, which can be accomplished by the `cv2.resize()` function. It takes image, scaling factor, and interpolation method as inputs.

The interpolation method parameter can have any one of the following values:

- `INTER_LINEAR`: This deals with bilinear interpolation (default value)
- `INTER_NEAREST`: This deals with the nearest-neighbor interpolation
- `INTER_AREA`: This is associated with resampling using pixel area relation (preferred for shrinking)
- `INTER_CUBIC` : This deals with bicubic interpolation over 4 x 4 pixel neighborhood (preferred for zooming)
- `INTER_LANCZOS4`: This deals with Lanczos interpolation over 8 x 8 pixel neighbourhood

The following example shows the usage for upscaling and downscaling:

```
import cv2
img = cv2.imread('/home/pi/book/test_set/house.tiff',1)
upscale = cv2.resize(img,None,fx=1.5,fy=1.5,
  interpolation=cv2.INTER_CUBIC)
```

```
downscale = cv2.resize(img,None,fx=0.5,fy=0.5,
  interpolation=cv2.INTER_AREA)
cv2.imshow('upscale',UpScale)
cv2.waitKey(0)
cv2.imshow('downscale',DownScale)
cv2.waitKey(0)
cv2.destroyAllWindows()
```

In the preceding code, we upscale the image in the x and y axes with a factor of 1.5 and downscale in x and y axes with a factor of 0.5. Run the code and see the output for yourself.

Translation, rotation, and affine transformation

The `cv2.warpAffine()` function can be used to perform translation, rotation, and affine transformation. It takes an input image, transformation matrix, and size of the output image as inputs, and returns the transformed image.

You can read more about affine transformations at `http://mathworld.wolfram.com/AffineTransformation.html`.

The following examples show different types of transformations which can be implemented with `cv.warpAffine()`.

Translation means shifting the location of the image. The shifting factor in (x,y) can be denoted with the transformation matrix, as follows:

$$T = \begin{bmatrix} 1 & 0 & x \\ 0 & 1 & y \end{bmatrix}$$

The following code shifts the location of the image with (-50,50):

```
import numpy as np
import cv2
import matplotlib.pyplot as plt

img = cv2.imread('/home/pi/book/test_set/house.tiff',1)
input=cv2.cvtColor(img,cv2.COLOR_BGR2RGB)
```

```
rows,cols,channel = img.shape

T = np.float32([[1,0,-50],[0,1,50]])
output = cv2.warpAffine(input,T,(cols,rows))

plt.imshow ( output ) , plt.title ('Shifted Image')
plt.show()
```

The output is shown as follows:

Some parts of the image will be cropped as the size of the output is the same as the input.

Similarly, we can use `cv2.warpAffine()` to apply scaled rotation to an image. For this, we need to define a rotation matrix with the use of `cv2.getRotationMatrix2D()`, which accepts the center of the rotation, the angle of anti-clockwise rotation (in degrees), and the scale as parameters, and provides a rotation matrix, which can be specified as the parameter to `cv2.warpAffine()`.

The following example rotates the image by 45 degrees with the center of the image as the center of rotation, and scales it down to 50% of the original image:

```
import cv2
import matplotlib.pyplot as plt

img = cv2.imread('/home/pi/book/test_set/house.tiff',1)
input=cv2.cvtColor(img,cv2.COLOR_BGR2RGB)
rows,cols,channel = img.shape

R = cv2.getRotationMatrix2D((cols/2,rows/2),45,0.5)
output = cv2.warpAffine(input,R,(cols,rows))

plt.imshow ( output ) , plt.title ('Rotated and Downscaled Image')
plt.show()
```

The output will be as follows:

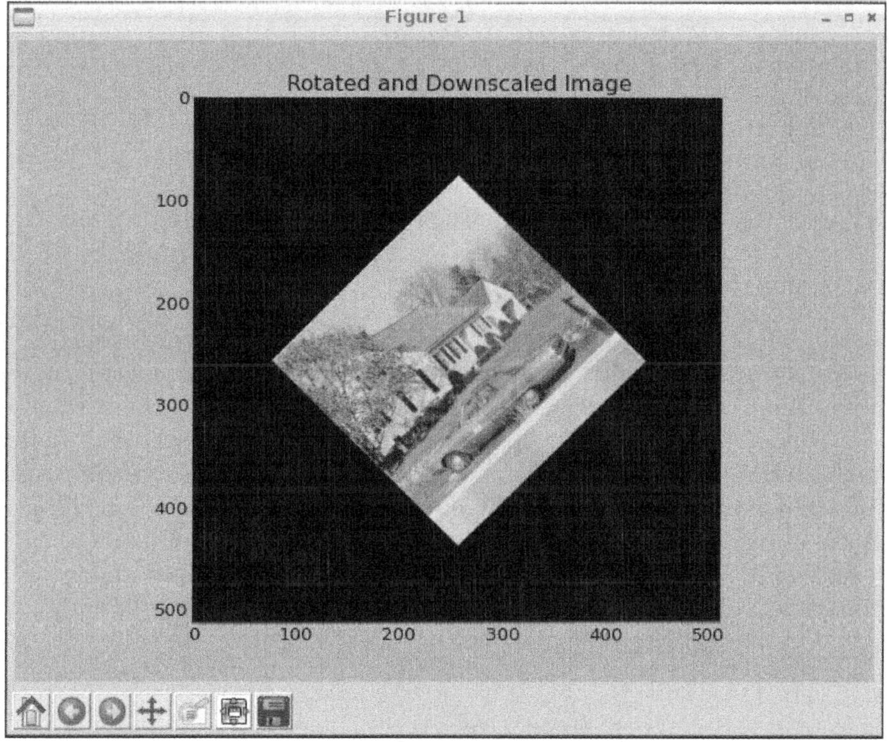

We can create some animation / visual effects by changing the rotation angle at regular intervals and then displaying it in a continuous loop till the *Esc* key is pressed. Following is the code for this (check the output yourself):

```
import cv2
from time import sleep

image = cv2.imread('/home/pi/book/test_set/house.tiff',1)
rows,cols,channels = image.shape

angle = 0
while(1):

  if angle == 360:
    angle=0

  M = cv2.getRotationMatrix2D((cols/2,rows/2),angle,1)
  rotated = cv2.warpAffine(image,M,(cols,rows))
  cv2.imshow('Rotating Image',rotated)
  angle=angle+1
  sleep(0.2)
  if cv2.waitKey(1) == 27 :
    break

cv2.destroyAllWindows()
```

Try implementing this on the live cam for more fun.

Next, we will see how to implement an affine transformation on any image. An affine transformation is a function between affine spaces. After applying the affine transformation on an image, the parallelism between the lines in an image is preserved. This means that the parallel lines in original images remain parallel even after transformation. The affine transformation needs any three non-collinear points (points which are not on the same line) in the original image and the corresponding points in the transformed image. These points are passed as arguments to `cv2.getAffineTransform()` to get the transformation matrix, and that matrix, in turn, is passed to `cv2.warpAffine()` as an argument. Take a look at the following example:

```
import cv2
import numpy as np
from matplotlib import pyplot as plt
```

```
image = cv2.imread('/home/pi/book/test_set/2.1.11.tiff',1)

#changing the colorspace from  BGR->RGB
input = cv2.cvtColor(image, cv2.COLOR_BGR2RGB )

rows,cols,channels = input.shape

points1 = np.float32([[100,100],[300,100],[100,300]])
points2 = np.float32([[200,150],[400,150],[100,300]])

A = cv2.getAffineTransform(points1,points2)

output = cv2.warpAffine(input,A,(cols,rows))

plt.subplot(121),plt.imshow(input),plt.title('Input')
plt.subplot(122),plt.imshow(output),plt.title('Affine Output')
plt.show()
```

The output will appear as follows:

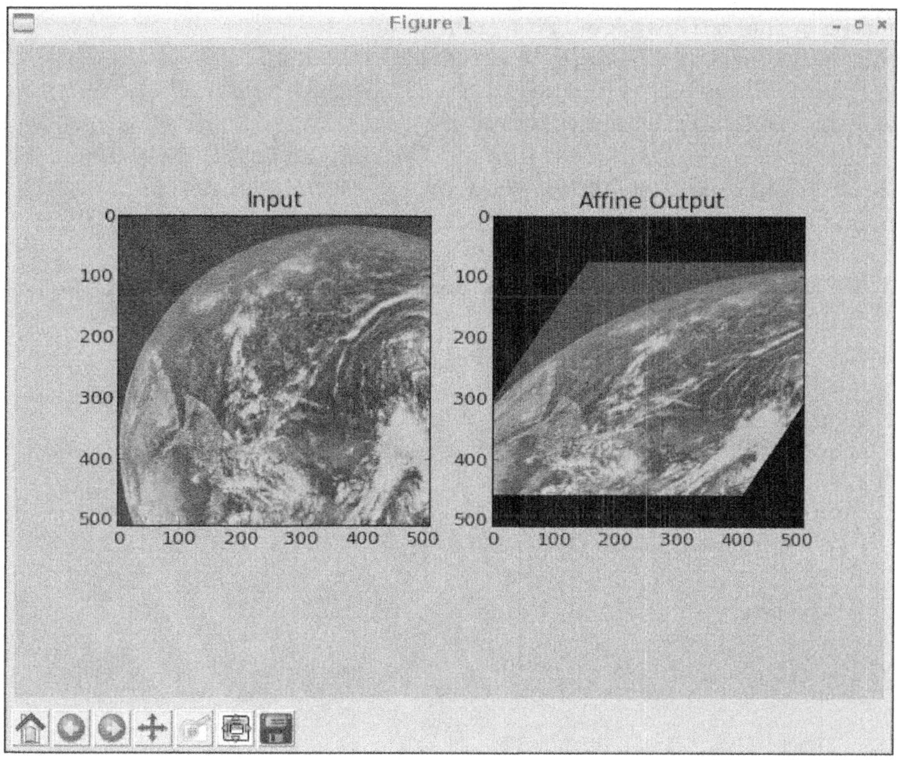

Perspective transformation

In perspective transformation, we provide four points from the input image and corresponding four points in the output image. The condition is that any three of these points should not be collinear (again, not in the same line). Like affine transformation, in perspective transformation, a straight line will remain straight. However, the parallelism between the lines will not be preserved. A real-life example of perspective transformation would be the zooming and angled zoom functionality in software. The degree and angle of zoom depends on the transformation matrix, which is defined by a set of four input and four output points. Let's see an example of the simple zoom functionality with the following code, where we use `cv2.getPerspectiveTransform()` to generate the transformation matrix and `cv2.warpPerspective()` to get the transformed output:

```
import cv2
import numpy as np
from matplotlib import pyplot as plt

image = cv2.imread('/home/pi/book/test_set/ruler.512.tiff',1)

#changing the colorspace from  BGR->RGB
input = cv2.cvtColor(image, cv2.COLOR_BGR2RGB )

rows,cols,channels = input.shape

points1 = np.float32([[0,0],[400,0],[0,400],[400,400]])
points2 = np.float32([[0,0],[300,0],[0,300],[300,300]])

P = cv2.getPerspectiveTransform(points1,points2)

output = cv2.warpPerspective(input,P,(300,300))

plt.subplot(121),plt.imshow(input),plt.title('Input')
plt.subplot(122),plt.imshow(output),plt.title('Perspective
  Transform')
plt.show()
```

The output will appear as follows:

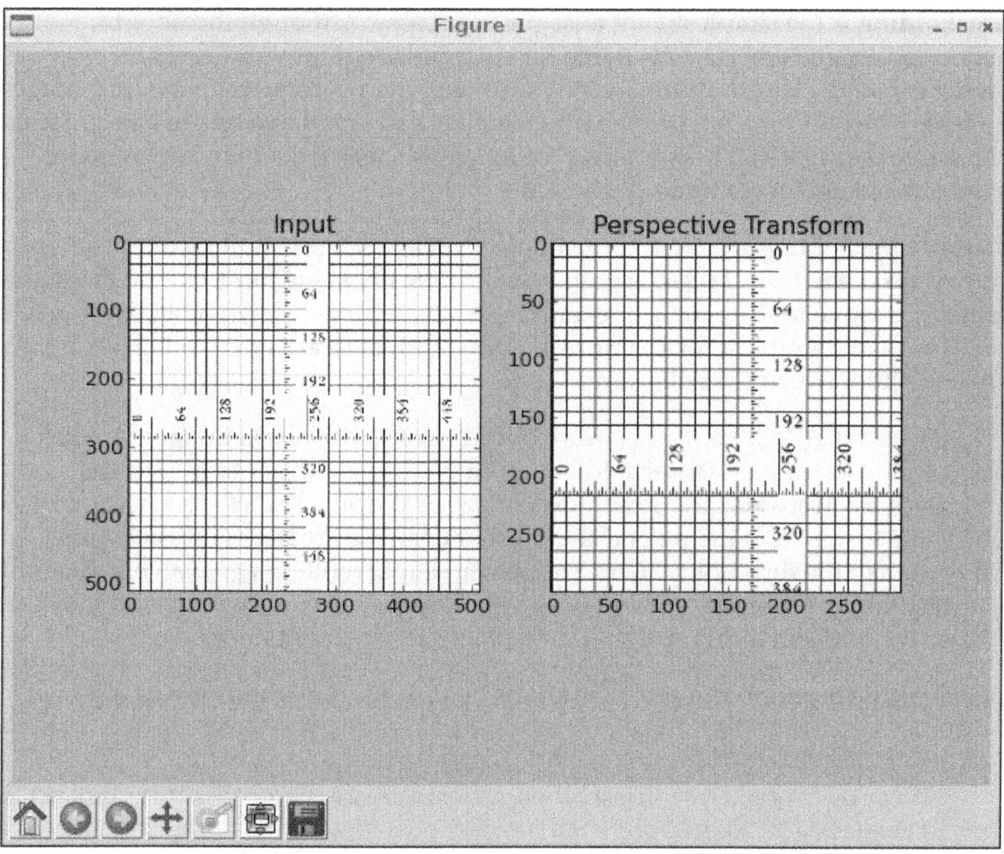

Try passing various combination of the parameters to see how the resultant image changes. In the preceding example, parallelism between the lines is preserved because of the combination of the parameters we used. You might want to try different combinations of the parameters to see that the parallelism between the lines is not preserved.

Thresholding image

Thresholding is the simplest way to segment images. Although thresholding methods and algorithms are available for colored images, it works best on grayscale images. Thresholding usually (but not always) converts grayscale images into binary images (in a binary image, each pixel can only have one of two possible values: white or black). Thresholding the image is usually the first step in many image processing applications.

The way thresholding works is very simple. We define a threshold value. For a pixel in a grayscale image, if the value of grayscale intensity is greater than the threshold, we assign a value to the pixel (for example, white), else we assign a black value to the pixel. This is the simplest form of thresholding and there are many other variations of this method, which we will see now.

In OpenCV, the `cv2.threshold()` function is used to threshold images. It takes as input, grayscale image, threshold value, `maxVal`, and threshold method as parameters, and returns the thresholded image as output. The `maxVal` parameter is the value assigned to the pixel if the pixel intensity is greater (or less in some methods) than the threshold. There are five threshold methods available in OpenCV; in the beginning, the simplest form of thresholding we saw is `cv2.THRESH_BINARY`. Let's see the mathematical representation of all the threshold methods.

Say (x,y) is the input pixel; then, operations by threshold methods are as follows:

- `cv2.THRESH_BINARY`

  If `intensity(x,y)` > thresh, then set `intensity(x,y)` = `maxVal`; else set `intensity(x,y)` = 0.

- `cv2.THRESH_BINARY_INV`

  If `intensity(x,y)` > thresh, then set `intensity(x,y)` = 0; else set `intensity(x,y)` = `maxVal`.

- `cv2.THRESH_TRUNC`

  If `intensity(x,y)` > thresh, then set `intensity(x,y)`=threshold; else leave `intensity(x,y)` as it is.

- `cv2.THRESH_TOZERO`

  If `intensity(x,y)` > thresh; then leave `intensity(x,y)` as it is; else set `intensity(x,y)` = 0.

- `cv2.THRESH_TOZERO_INV`

  If `intensity(x,y)` > thresh, then set `intensity(x,y)` = 0; else leave `intensity(x,y)` as it is.

The demonstration of the threshold functionality usually works best on grayscale images with a gradually increasing gradient. In the following example, we chose the value of the threshold as 127, so the image is segmented into two sets of pixels depending on the value of their intensity:

```
import cv2
import matplotlib.pyplot as plt

img = cv2.imread('/home/pi/book/test_set/gray21.512.tiff',0)
th=127
max_val=255
ret,o1 = cv2.threshold(img,th,max_val,cv2.THRESH_BINARY)
ret,o2 = cv2.threshold(img,th,max_val,cv2.THRESH_BINARY_INV)
ret,o3 = cv2.threshold(img,th,max_val,cv2.THRESH_TOZERO)
ret,o4 = cv2.threshold(img,th,max_val,cv2.THRESH_TOZERO_INV)
ret,o5 = cv2.threshold(img,th,max_val,cv2.THRESH_TRUNC)

titles = ['Input Image','BINARY','BINARY_INV','TOZERO','TOZERO_
INV','TRUNC']
output = [img, o1, o2, o3, o4, o5]

for i in xrange(6):
    plt.subplot(2,3,i+1),plt.imshow(output[i],cmap='gray')
    plt.title(titles[i])
    plt.xticks([]),plt.yticks([])
plt.show()
```

The output of the code will appear as follows:

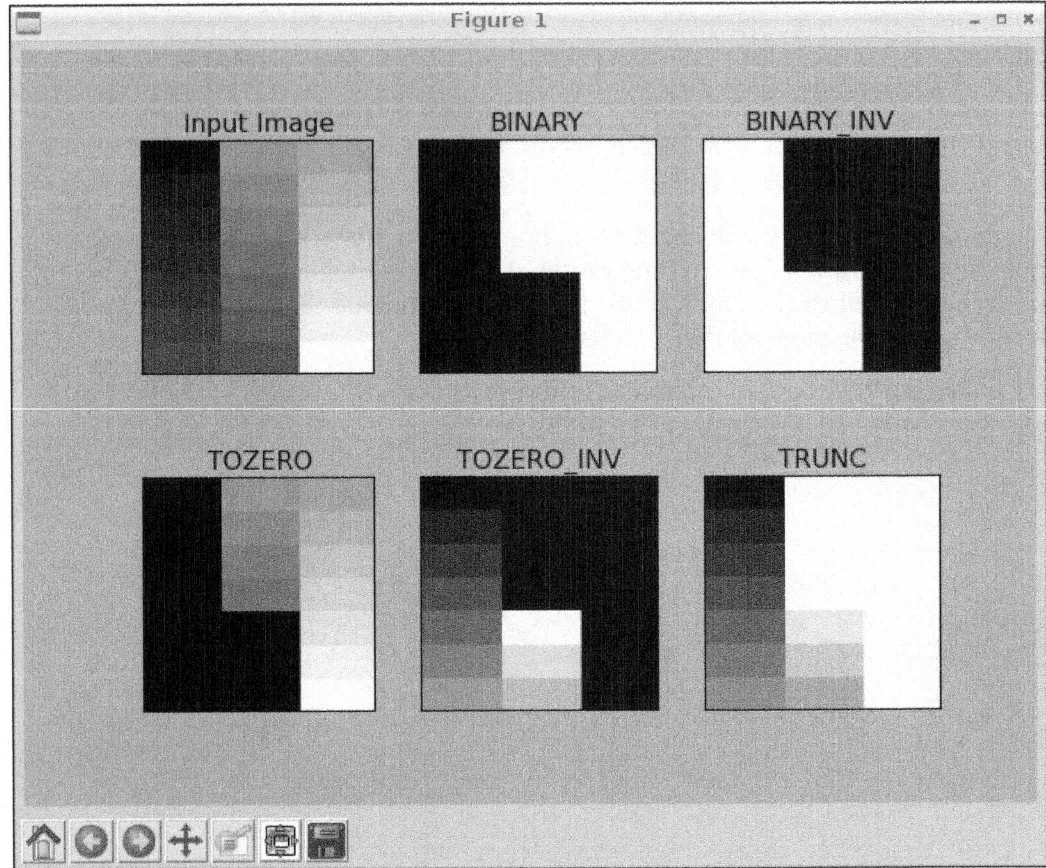

Otsu's method

Otsu's method for thresholding automatically determines the value of the threshold for the images, which have two peaks in their histogram (bi-modal histograms). This usually means the image has background and foreground pixels, and Otsu's method is the best way to separate these two sets of pixels automatically without specifying the threshold value.

Otsu's method is not the best way for images which are not in the background + foreground model, and they may provide improper output if applied. This method is applied in addition to other methods and the threshold is passed as 0. Try implementing the following code:

```
ret,output=cv2.threshold(image,0,255,cv2.
  THRESH_BINARY+cv2.THRESH_OTSU)
```

The output of this will be as follows. This is an image of a tank in a desert:

Exercise

Explore `cv2.adaptiveThreshold()`, which is used for adaptive thresholding of images based on uneven lighting conditions (some parts of the image are more illuminated than others).

Summary

In this chapter, we explored colorspaces and its applications in image tracking with one color and multiple colors. Then, we applied transformations on images. Finally, we saw how to threshold an image.

In the next chapter, we will go over the basics of noise and filtering the noise, as well as smoothening/blurring images with Low Pass Filters.

5
Let's Make Some Noise

In the previous chapter, we learned about colorspace conversion, transformations, and threshold. In this chapter, we will learn about the basics of noise in images and low-pass filtering techniques. Here are the topics that we will explore in this chapter:

- The basics of noise and the introducing of salt-and-pepper noise to an image
- Kernel and low-pass filters
- Low-pass filtering techniques

Noise

Noise means any unwanted signal. Image/video noise signifies unwanted variations in the intensity (for grayscale image) or color (for color images) that is not present in the real object that was photographed or recorded. Image noise is a form of electronic disruption, and it can come from many sources, such as camera sensors and circuitry in digital or analog cameras. Noise in digital cameras is the equivalent of the film grain of analog cameras. Though some noise is always present in any output of electronic devices, a high amount of image noise considerably degrades the overall image quality, making it useless for the intended purpose. To represent the quality of electronic output (in our case, digital images), the mathematical term **signal-to-noise ratio** (**SNR**) is very useful. Mathematically, it's defined as follows:

$$SNR = \frac{SignalPower}{NoisePower}$$

A higher signal-to-noise ratio translates into a better quality image.

Introducing noise to an image

As we have seen earlier, noise can be introduced from many components in a camera, which include the lens, sensors, or the circuitry itself. We can simulate the noise by introducing it ourselves. Salt-and-pepper noise means the random appearance of black (pepper) and white (salt) pixels in the image. The following example shows how to add salt-and-pepper noise into the Lena image:

```
import numpy as np
import cv2
import random
import matplotlib.pyplot as plt

img = cv2.imread('/home/pi/book/test_set/lena_color_512.tif',1)
input = cv2.cvtColor(img,cv2.COLOR_BGR2RGB)
output = np.zeros(input.shape,np.uint8)
p = 0.05 # probablity of noise
for i in range (input.shape[0]):
  for j in range(input.shape[1]):
    r = random.random()
    if r < p/2:
      output[i][j] = 0,0,0
    elif r < p:
      output[i][j] = 255,255,255
    else:
      output[i][j] = input[i][j]

plt.imshow(output), plt.title('Salt and Pepper Sprinkled')
plt.xticks([]),plt.yticks([])
plt.show()
```

In the preceding program, we set the noise density (*p*) to `0.05` and generated a random number for each pixel. If the random number is less than *p/2*, we set the pixel to black (pepper), if it's greater than *p/2* but less than *p*, we set it to white (salt). Otherwise, we leave the pixel untouched. Finally, we used matplotlib to display the image with noise.

The output image will be different every time we run the code since the noise is added randomly using the `random.random()` function. The following screenshot is of one of the outputs:

Kernels

In the following concepts and their implementations, we are going to use kernels. Kernels are square matrices used in some image processing operations. We can apply a kernel to an image to get different results, such as blurring, smoothing, edge detection, and sharpening of an image. One of the main uses of kernels is to apply a low-pass filter to an image. Low-pass filters average out the rapid changes in the intensity of image pixels. This basically smoothens or blurs the image. A simple averaging kernel can be mathematically represented as follows:

$$K = \frac{All\ Ones\ Matrix}{Rows * Cols}$$

For row = cols = 3, *K* will be as follows:

$$K = \frac{\begin{bmatrix} 1 & 1 & 1 \\ 1 & 1 & 1 \\ 1 & 1 & 1 \end{bmatrix}}{9}$$

The value of rows and columns is always odd.

We can use the following NumPy code to create this kernel:

```
K=np.ones((3,3),np.uint32)/9
```

2D convolution filtering

The `cv2.filter2D()` function convolves the aforementioned kernel with the image, thus applying a linear filter to the image. This function accepts the source image and the depth of the destination image (`-1` in our case; `-1` means the same depth as the source image) and a kernel. Have a look at the following code. It applies a 7x7 averaging filter to an image:

```
import cv2
import numpy as np
from matplotlib import pyplot as plt

img = cv2.imread('/home/pi/book/test_set/4.2.03.tiff',1)

input = cv2.cvtColor(img,cv2.COLOR_BGR2RGB)
output = cv2.filter2D(input,-1,np.ones((7,7),np.float32)/49)
```

```
plt.subplot(121),plt.imshow(input),plt.title('Input')
plt.xticks([]), plt.yticks([])
plt.subplot(122),plt.imshow(output),plt.title('Output')
plt.xticks([]), plt.yticks([])
plt.show()
```

The output will be a filtered image, as follows:

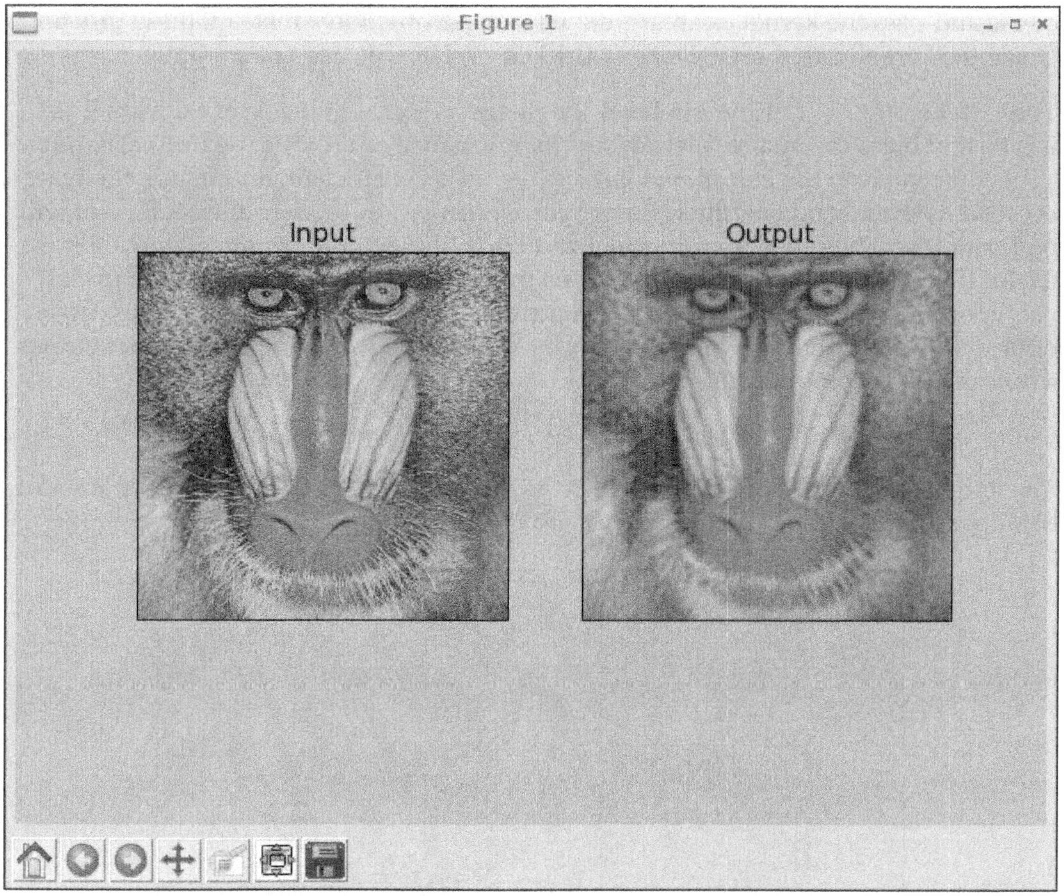

You can find interactive tutorials on convolution at the following URL: http://micro.magnet.fsu.edu/primer/java/digitalimaging/processing/kernelmaskoperation/

Low-pass filtering

As discussed in the section on kernels, low-pass filters are excellent if you wish to remove sharp components (high-frequency information), such as edges and noise, and retain low-frequency information (the so-called low-pass filters), thus blurring or smoothening them.

Let's explore the low-pass filtering functions available in OpenCV. We do not have to create and pass the kernel as an argument to these functions. Instead, these functions create the kernel, based on the size of the kernel that we pass as a parameter.

The `cv2.boxFilter()` function takes the image, `ddepth`, and size of the kernel as inputs and blurs the image. We can specify normalize as either `true` or `false`. If it's `True`, the matrix in the kernel will have $\frac{1}{rows * cols}$ as it's coefficient, and hence, the matrix is called a normalized box filter. If normalize is set to `False`, then the coefficient will be 1, and it will be called an unnormalized box filter. An unnormalized box filter is useful if you want to compute the various integral characteristics over each pixel neighborhood, such as the covariance matrices of image derivatives (used in dense optical flow algorithms and many other instances).The following code demonstrates the normalized box filter:

```
output=cv2.boxFilter(input,-1,(3,3),normalize=True)
```

The output of the preceding code will be as follows, and it will have a lesser amount of smoothing than the previous one due to the size of the kernel matrix:

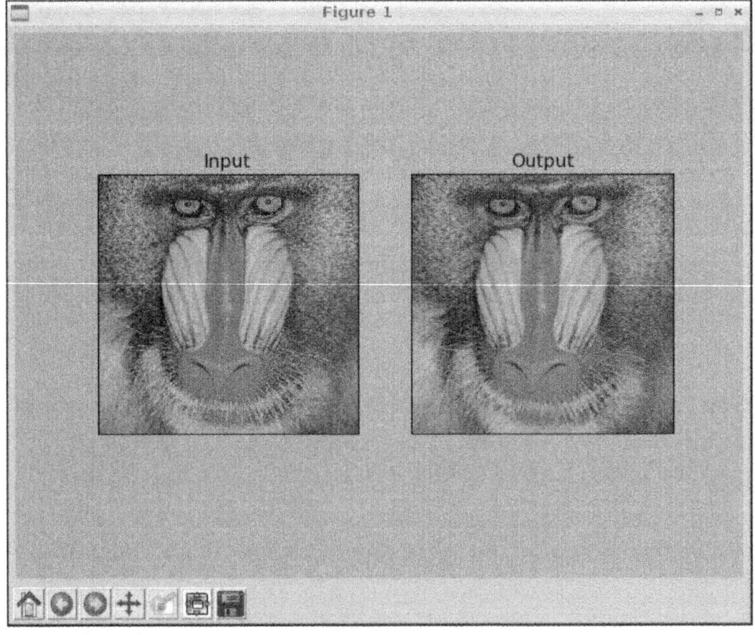

The `cv2.blur()` function directly provides the normalized box filter by accepting the input image and kernel size as parameters without the need to specify the `normalize` parameter. The output for the following code will be exactly the same as the preceding output:

```
output = cv2.blur(input,(3,3))
```

As an exercise, try passing normalize as `False` for an unnormalised box filter to `cv2.boxFilter()` and see the output.

The `cv2.GaussianBlur()` function uses the Gaussian kernel in place of a box filter to apply. This filter is highly effective against Gaussian noise. The following is the code that you can use to implement this function:

```
output = cv2.GaussianBlur(input,(3,3),0)
```

You may want to read more about Gaussian Noise at `http://homepages.inf.ed.ac.uk/rbf/HIPR2/noise.htm`.

The following is the output of the preceding code where the input is an image with Gaussian noise and the output is the image with the Gaussian noise removed:

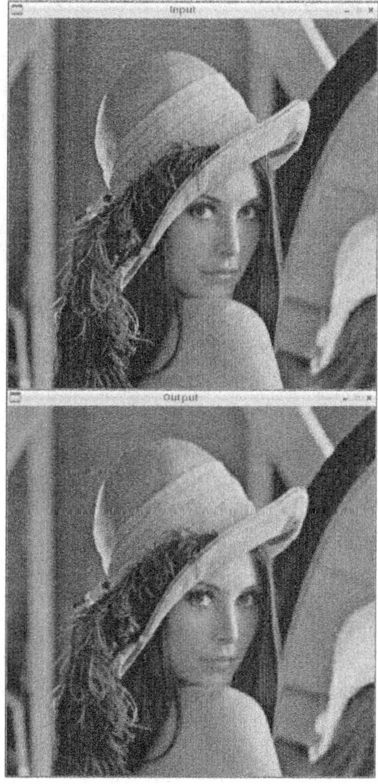

The `cv2.medianBlur()` function is used for the median blurring of an image using the median filter. It calculates the median of all the values under the kernel, and the centre pixel in the kernel is replaced with the calculated medium. In this filter, a window slides along the image, and the median intensity value of the pixels within the window becomes the output intensity of the pixel being processed. It's highly effective against salt-and-pepper noise. We need to pass an input image and an odd positive integer (not the rows, columns tuple like the previous two functions) to this function. The following code introduces salt-and-pepper noise in the image and then applies the `cv2.medianBlur()` function to that to remove the noise:

```
import cv2
import numpy as np
import random
from matplotlib import pyplot as plt

img = cv2.imread('/home/pi/book/test_set/lena_color_512.tif',1)

input = cv2.cvtColor(img,cv2.COLOR_BGR2RGB)

output = np.zeros(input.shape,np.uint8)
p = 0.2 # probablity of noise
for i in range (input.shape[0]):
  for j in range(input.shape[1]):
    r = random.random()
    if r < p/2:
      output[i][j] = 0,0,0
    elif r < p:
      output[i][j] = 255,255,255
    else:
      output[i][j] = input[i][j]

noise_removed = cv2.medianBlur(output,3)

plt.subplot(121),plt.imshow(output),plt.title('Noisy Image')
plt.xticks([]), plt.yticks([])
plt.subplot(122),plt.imshow(noise_removed),plt.title('Median
Filtering')
plt.xticks([]), plt.yticks([])
plt.show()
```

You will find out that the salt-and-pepper noise has been drastically reduced and the image is much more comprehensible to the human eye:

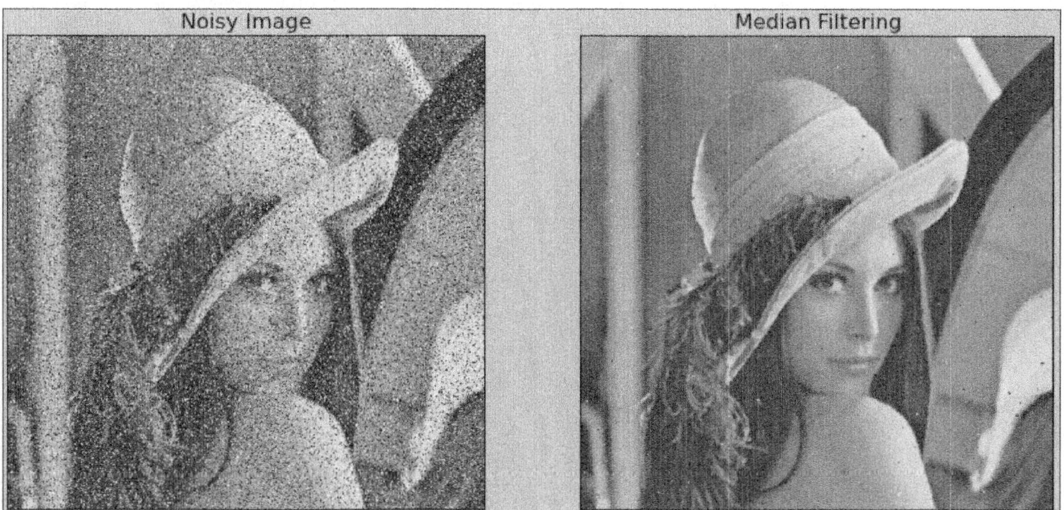

Exercise

As an exercise for this chapter, explore `cv2.sepFilter2D()`, which is used for separable linear filtering. Also, explore the `cv2.BilateralFilter()` filter function that filters noise while keeping the edges sharp. You may want to find out the mathematics behind the Gaussian noise.

Summary

In this chapter, we learned about noise as well as low-pass filtering techniques used to smooth images. In the next chapter, we will study high-pass filtering techniques and the detection of edges using the Canny Edge detection algorithm. We will also write programs to detect circles and lines using Hough's Transforms in a live video from a webcam.

6
Edges, Circles, and Lines' Detection

In the last chapter, you learned about noise and how you can introduce it in an image. Then, you studied kernels, low-pass filters, and the applications of these filters in the blurring, smoothening, and denoising of images. In this chapter, you will study the different types of high-pass filters and their applications. You will also see how to use the Canny Edge detection method on images. Finally, we will cover how one can identify circles and lines in a live webcam feed. The following topics will be covered in this chapter:

- High-pass filters
- Laplacian, Sobel, and Scharr methods for high-pass filtering
- The Canny Edge detection algorithm and implementation
- Circle tracking and line tracking in a live video

High-pass filters

High-pass filtering (**HPF**) is exactly the opposite of low-pass filtering. In low-pass filtering, an image is usually blurred, whereas after applying high-pass filtering, an image is sharpened. All high-pass filters will let high frequency information like edges to enhance, while restricting low-frequency information (hence, they are called high-pass filters). These filters are also called derivative masks and are widely used in edge detection and extraction algorithms. Edge is an important type of feature in an image. We will study three derivative functions available in OpenCV and see how these are useful in the extracting of edges.

OpenCV provides the `Sobel()`, `Laplacian()`, and `Scharr()` functions for high-pass filtering.

You can read more about mathematics behind these functions on the web at the following URLs:

`http://www.tutorialspoint.com/dip/Sobel_operator.htm`

`http://www.tutorialspoint.com/dip/Laplacian_Operator.htm`

The following are the most common parameters used in the functions mentioned before:

- `src`: This is the source image.
- `ddepth`: This is the depth of the target image. `-1` stands for the same depth of target as that of the source. The following combinations of source image depth and target image depth are supported by `Laplacian()`, `Sobel()`, and `Scharr()` derivatives.

Source image depth	**Target image depth**
`CV_8U`	`-1/CV_16S/CV_32F/CV_64F`
`CV_16U/CV_16S`	`-1/CV_32F/CV_64F`
`CV_32F`	`-1/CV_32F/CV_64F`
`CV_64F`	`-1/CV_64F`

- `dx`: This is the order of the x derivative (not required for `Laplacian()`).
- `dy`: This is the order of the y derivative (not required for `Laplacian()`).
- `ksize`: This is the kernel size (1,3,5,7 for `sobel()`, a positive odd number for `Laplacian()`, and is not required for `Scharr()`).
- `scale`: This is the optional scale for computed derivative values.

- `delta`: This is the optional delta value that is added to the results prior to storing them in the output.
- `borderType`: This is the pixel extrapolation method for boundary pixels.

Let's see the code in action for `Sobel()`, `Laplacian()`, and `Scarr()`. In the following code, we will compute the Laplacian of the image as well as the first-order *x* derivative, using the `Scarr()` and `Sobel()` functions:

```
import cv2
import matplotlib.pyplot as plt

img = cv2.imread('/home/pi/book/test_set/1.3.12.tiff',0)

laplacian = cv2.Laplacian(img,ddepth=cv2.CV_32F,
  ksize=17,scale=1,delta=0,borderType=cv2.BORDER_DEFAULT)

sobel = cv2.Sobel(img,ddepth=cv2.CV_32F,dx=1,dy=0,
  ksize=11,scale=1,delta=0,borderType=cv2.BORDER_DEFAULT)

scharr = cv2.Scharr(img,ddepth=cv2.CV_32F,dx=1,dy=0,scale=1,
  delta=0,borderType=cv2.BORDER_DEFAULT)

images=[img,laplacian,sobel,scharr]

titles=['Original','Laplacian','Sobel','Scharr']

for i in xrange(4):
  plt.subplot(2,2,i+1)
  plt.imshow(images[i],cmap = 'gray')
  plt.title(titles[i]),
  plt.xticks([]), plt.yticks([])
plt.show()
```

The following screenshot depicts the output of the code. As you can see, the calculation of the x derivative of the image with `Sobel()` and `Scharr()` gives us the vertical borders of the original image:

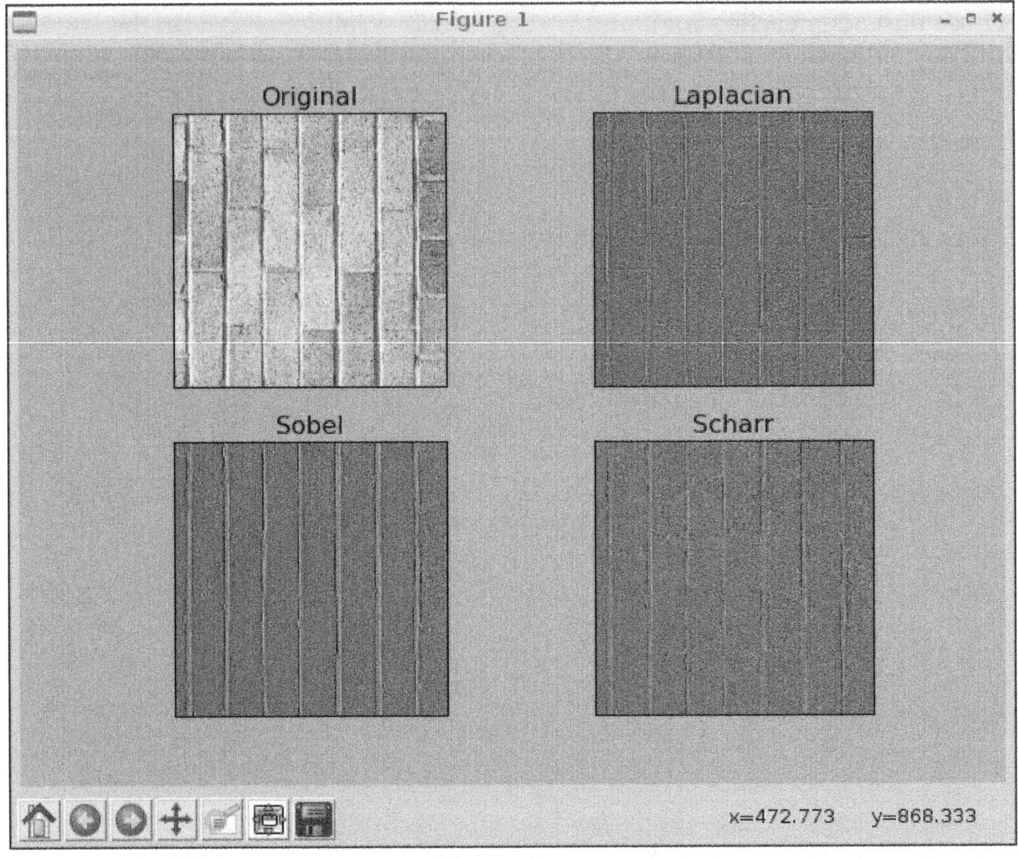

As an exercise, compute the first-order y derivatives of the image using the `Sobel` and `Scharr` functions. Then, use the `cv2.add()` function to add the Sobel x derivative to the Sobel y derivative. In the same way, add the Scharr x derivative to the Scharr y derivative of the same image and compare the results.

Canny Edge detector

The Canny Edge detector is a multistage edge detection method developed by John Canny.

The following links explain the Canny Edge detection in detail:

`http://dasl.mem.drexel.edu/alumni/bGreen/www.pages.drexel.edu/_weg22/can_tut.html`

`http://homepages.inf.ed.ac.uk/rbf/HIPR2/canny.htm`

OpenCV implements it using `cv2.Canny()`. It works in the following stages:

1. A Gaussian kernel is applied to filter out any noise. A 5x5 kernel is used.
2. The intensity gradient of the image is calculated. If L2gradient is true, then the L2 norm is used, and if it's false, then the L1 norm is used.
3. Non-maximum suppression is applied to the output of *step* 2 and the candidate edges are identified.
4. The final step involves hysteresis. The values of `threshold1` and `threshold2` are passed to the function. Anything with a gradient below `threshold1` is excluded and anything with a gradient that is more than `threshold2` is included in the edge set. For the points in which the gradient lies between two thresholds, only the pixels that are connected to the pixels that lie above `threshold2` are accepted as part of the final edge set.

The following parameters are usually passed to `cv2.Canny()`:

- `img`: This is the input image.
- `threshold1`: This is the lower threshold.
- `threshold2`: This is the upper threshold.
- `L2gradient`: This is a Boolean value. If it's `True`, then the L2 norm is used. Otherwise, the L1 norm is used to calculate the gradient. Usually, the L2 norm is more accurate than the L1 norm, but the former requires more time for computation.

The function will return a set with the detected edges.

The following code will compute and display the edges with the help of the Canny detector:

```
import cv2
import matplotlib.pyplot as plt

img = cv2.imread('/home/pi/book/test_set/house.tif',0)
edges1 = cv2.Canny(img,50,300,L2gradient=False)
edges2 = cv2.Canny(img,100,150,L2gradient=True)

images = [img,edges1,edges2]
titles = ['Original','L1 Gradient','L2 Gradient']

for i in xrange(3):
  plt.subplot(1,3,i+1)
  plt.imshow(images[i],cmap = 'gray')
  plt.title(titles[i]),
  plt.xticks([]), plt.yticks([])
plt.show()
```

The output will be as follows:

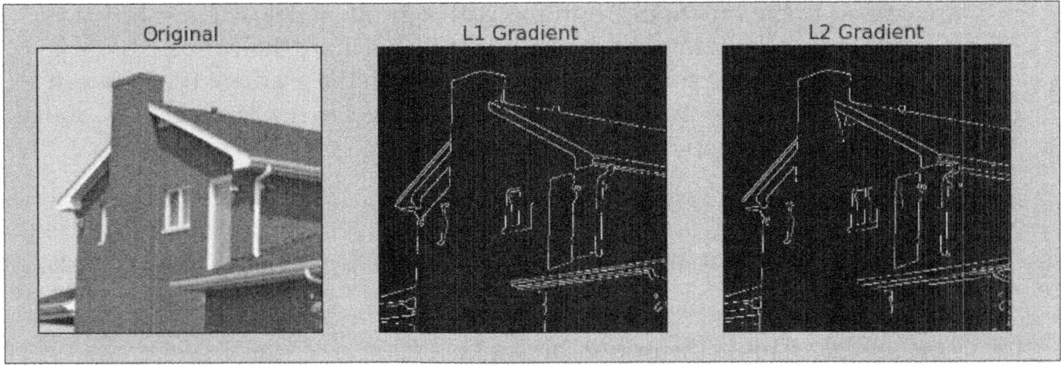

As an exercise, try to run the above program with different combinations of parameters.

Hough circle and line transforms

OpenCV has `cv2.HoughCircles()` to detect the circle feature in an image, and it returns the circles in the images in the form of a vector (*x*, *y*, *radius*).

You can find the details with regard to the mathematics behind the Hough circle transform at the following URL:

http://docs.opencv.org/doc/tutorials/imgproc/imgtrans/hough_circle/hough_circle.html

It accepts the following parameters as arguments:

- An image: This is an 8-bit single-channel grayscale.
- The detection method: This is the method for circle detection. As of now, only one method, `cv2.cv.CV_HOUGH_GRADIENT`, has been implemented.
- *dp*: This is the inverse ratio of resolution. This is the formula:

$$dp = \frac{(\text{image resolution})}{(\text{accumulator resolution})}$$

- `minDist`: This is the minimum distance between the centers of the detected circles.
- `param1` and `param2`: These are the method-specific parameters. The `param1` method is the highest threshold of the underlying Canny method, and the `param2` method is the accumulator threshold for `CV_HOUGH_GRADIENT`.
- `minRadius` and `maxRadius`: These are the respective parameters for the minimum and maximum radius of the circles for detection.

The following program accepts the feed from the webcam and then smoothens the image by blurring it, before passing it to `cv2.HoughCircles()`. The detected circles are drawn using `cv2.Circle()`, which is something that we have already seen in *Chapter 2, Working with Images, Webcams, and GUI*:

```
import cv2

cam = cv2.VideoCapture(0)

while (True):
  ret , frame = cam.read()

  grey = cv2.cvtColor(frame,cv2.COLOR_BGR2GRAY)
  blur = cv2.blur(grey,(5,5))
```

```
        circles = cv2.HoughCircles(blur,
          method=cv2.cv.CV_HOUGH_GRADIENT,dp=1,minDist=200,
        param1=50,param2=13,minRadius=30,maxRadius=175)

  if circles is not None:
          for i in circles [0,:]:
                  cv2.circle(frame,(i[0],i[1]),i[2],(0,255,0),2)
                  cv2.circle(frame,(i[0],i[1]),2,(0,0,255),3)

  cv2.imshow('Detected',frame)
  if cv2.waitKey(5) == 27:
    break

cv2.destroyAllWindows()
cam.release()
```

I used this program on two coins and a round magnet placed on my desk. The program works very well and detects all the round objects. The output is as follows:

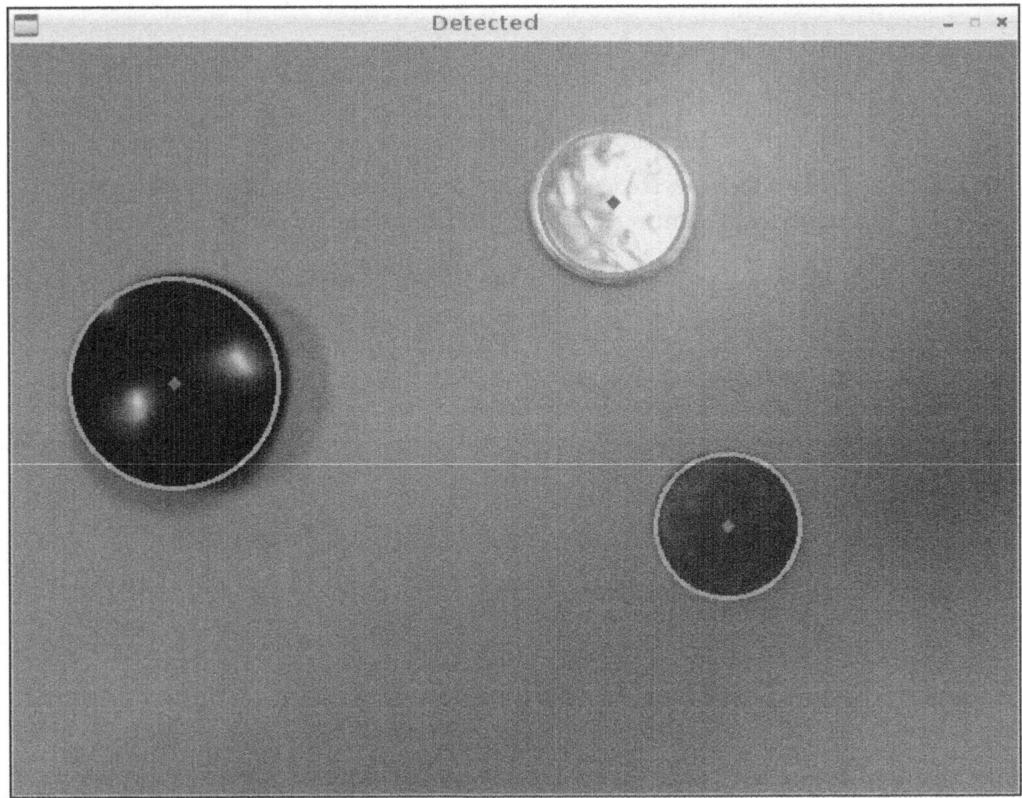

OpenCV also has a `cv2.HoughLines()` function to find the lines. Let's see how we can detect lines in a live video feed.

In the following example, `cv2.HoughLines()` accepts the following parameters:

- An image: This is an 8-bit single-channel grayscale image
- The rho value: This is the distance accuracy of an accumulator
- The theta value: This is the angle accuracy of an accumulator
- The threshold: This is the accumulator threshold parameter

This function returns lines in the (*rho,theta*) vector that we need to convert to the (*x1,y1*),(*x2,y2*) system:

```
import numpy as np
import cv2

cam = cv2.VideoCapture(0)

while (1):

  ret, img = cam.read()
  gray = cv2.cvtColor(img,cv2.COLOR_BGR2GRAY)
  edges = cv2.Canny(gray,50,250,apertureSize=5,L2gradient=True)

  lines = cv2.HoughLines(edges,1,np.pi/180,200)

  if lines is not None:
    for rho,theta in lines[0]:
          a = np.cos(theta)
          b = np.sin(theta)
          x0 = a*rho
          y0 = b*rho
          pts1 = ( int(x0 + 1000*(-b)) , int(y0 + 1000*(a)) )
          pts2 = ( int(x0 - 1000*(-b)) , int(y0 - 1000*(a)) )
          cv2.line(img,pts1,pts2,(0,0,255),2)

  cv2.imshow('Detected Lines',img)
  if cv2.waitKey(1)  == 27:
              break

cv2.destroyAllWindows()
cam.release()
```

Run the preceding program and check the output yourself. The Hough transform functions have to be tuned for the given sample set. So, if you cannot see any circles and lines in your video or if there are a lot of false positives (that is, the programs detect circles and lines even when they are not present in the input frame), you might want to play a bit with the parameters to tune them according to your sample input to get the desired results.

Exercise

OpenCV has a `cv2.HoughLinesP` method that uses probabilistic Hough line transform to find the lines. The `cv2.cornerHarris()`, `cv2.goodFeaturesToTrack()`, and `cv2.FastFeatureDetector()` methods are used to detect the corners in an image. Explore these functions by yourself in more detail.

Summary

In this chapter, we saw how to apply high-pass filters to an image. We also explored and implemented the algorithms for the detection of features like edges, lines, and circles in OpenCV.

In our next chapter, we will explore image restoration, segmentation, quantization, and depth map in detail and write programs to implement these topics.

7
Image Restoration, Quantization, and Depth Map

In the previous chapter, we explored how to use high-pass filters to detect high-frequency features like edges in an image. We also explored its application in the Canny Edge detecting algorithm. In this chapter, we will explore a few more diverse techniques on images, including the following topics:

- Image restoration using inpainting
- Image segmentation
- Image quantization
- Depth estimation in stereo images

Restoring images using inpainting

Image restoration is the process of reconstructing the damaged parts of an image. There are different reasons as to why parts of an image can get damaged. For example, a photograph taken with a film camera and developed on photographic paper can get damaged over the years due to the deterioration of the storage media (in this case, the photographic paper). Small errors may be introduced in an image due to faulty sensors. In digital images, data errors can be introduced in an image during the transmission and reception. For example, when images are transmitted byte by byte (instead of packets), it is not feasible to use modern error checking and corrective networking protocols, which increase the probability of getting erroneous data. Many of these degraded images can be restored using the image inpainting technique. There are several algorithms available for the same, and OpenCV offers two of these with its `cv2.inpaint()` function.

It accepts a source image, an inpaint mask that is a grayscale image representation of the damaged area where the nonzero (white) pixels denote the area to be inpainted, an inpaint neighborhood side, and an algorithm that has to be applied as parameters. The function then returns the inpainted image. The following code demonstrates the implementation of both of these methods that are available in OpenCV for inpainting. The results are almost the same in both the algorithms. I manually created the damage and the corresponding mask (by inverting the damage pixels) in one of the paint software:

```
import cv2
import matplotlib.pyplot as plt

image = cv2.imread('/home/pi/book/test_set/DamagedImage.tiff')
mask = cv2.imread('/home/pi/book/test_set/Mask.tiff',0)

input = cv2.cvtColor ( image , cv2.COLOR_BGR2RGB )

output_TELEA = cv2.inpaint(input,mask,5,cv2.INPAINT_TELEA)
output_NS = cv2.inpaint(input,mask,5,cv2.INPAINT_NS)

plt.subplot(221),plt.imshow(input),plt.title('Damaged
  Image'),plt.xticks([]),plt.yticks([])
plt.subplot(222),plt.imshow(mask,cmap='gray'),
  plt.title('Mask'),plt.xticks([]),plt.yticks([])
plt.subplot(223),plt.imshow(output_TELEA),plt.title
  ('Telea Method'),plt.xticks([]),plt.yticks([])
plt.subplot(224),plt.imshow(output_NS),plt.title
  ('Navier Stokes Method'),plt.xticks([]),plt.yticks([])
plt.show()
```

In the preceding code, `cv2.INPAINT_TELEA` is based on a paper, *An Image Inpainting Technique Based on the Fast Marching Method* by *Alexandru Telea* that was published in 2004, and `cv2.INPAINT_NS` is based on a paper, *Navier-Stokes, Fluid Dynamics, and Image and Video Inpainting*, by *Bertalmio, Marcelo, Andrea L. Bertozzi*, and *Guillermo Sapiro* that was published in 2001.

The following is the output of the preceding code:

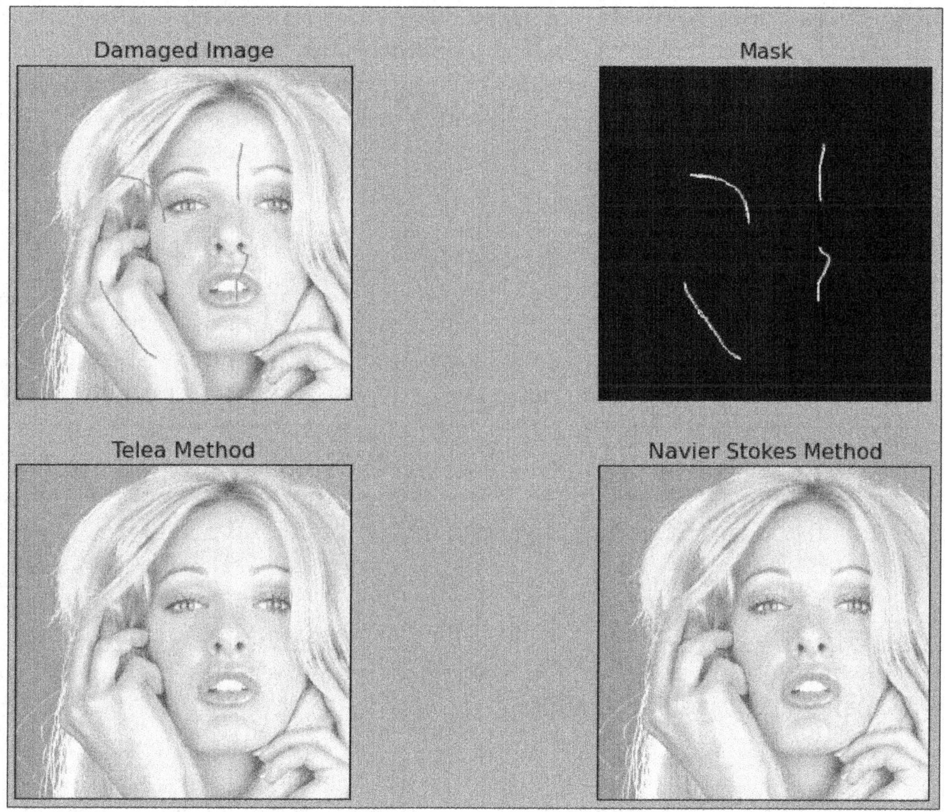

[You can find more details about image inpainting here:
http://www.math.ucla.edu/~imagers/htmls/inp.html]

Image segmentation

Image segmentation is the process of dividing images into multiple, relevant sections or parts based on some criteria. Thresholding the image can be considered the simplest form of segmentation, which we have already explored in *Chapter 4, Colorspaces, Transformations, and Thresholds*. We will cover two more segmentation methods in this chapter.

Mean shift algorithm based segmentation

The mean shift algorithm and its C++ implementation were developed by *Chris M. Christoudias* and *Bogdan Georgescu*. PyMeanShift is the Python extension to this algorithm. It uses NumPy arrays, making it compatible with OpenCV and other image processing extensions in Python like PIL/pillow.

You can find out more information about this on the project website, `https://code.google.com/p/pymeanshift/`. A link to the one of the forks of PyMeanShift on GitHub is `https://github.com/clememic/pymeanshift`.

As of now, no binary package is available for Unix, Linux, and their variants. So, we have to build and install it from the source. Download the latest version from `https://code.google.com/p/pymeanshift/downloads/list` using the `wget` utility. The file downloaded will be a `tar.gz` file. Copy it to the home folder and extract it. Then, navigate to the directory where you extracted the source code using the LXTerminal and run the following commands to build and install it:

```
sudo ./setup.py build
sudo ./setup.py install
```

Once the installation succeeds without any errors, input the following statement in the python interactive shell to test it:

```
import pymeanshift as pms
```

The PyMeanShift module provides the `pms.segment()` function, which is used for image segmentation. It takes the image to be segmented, and spatial radius, range radius, and minimum density as parameters, and it returns a segmented image, a segmented and color labeled image, and a number of regions. The following code demonstrates the use of this function:

```
import cv2
import numpy as np
import pymeanshift as pms
from matplotlib import pyplot as plt

image = cv2.imread('/home/pi/book/test_set/coins1.png',1)

#changing the colorspace from  BGR->RGB
input = cv2.cvtColor(image, cv2.COLOR_BGR2RGB )
```

```
(segmented_image, labels_image, number_regions) = pms.segment(
  input,spatial_radius=2,range_radius=2,min_density=300)


plt.subplot(131),plt.imshow(input),plt.title('Input')
plt.xticks([]),plt.yticks([])
plt.subplot(132),plt.imshow(segmented_image),plt.title(
  'Segmented Output')
plt.xticks([]),plt.yticks([])
plt.subplot(133),plt.imshow(labels_image),plt.title(
  'Labeled Output')
plt.xticks([]),plt.yticks([])
plt.show()
```

I took a picture of some coins of different denominations with picamera and used the same image as an input for this program. The output of the program is as follows:

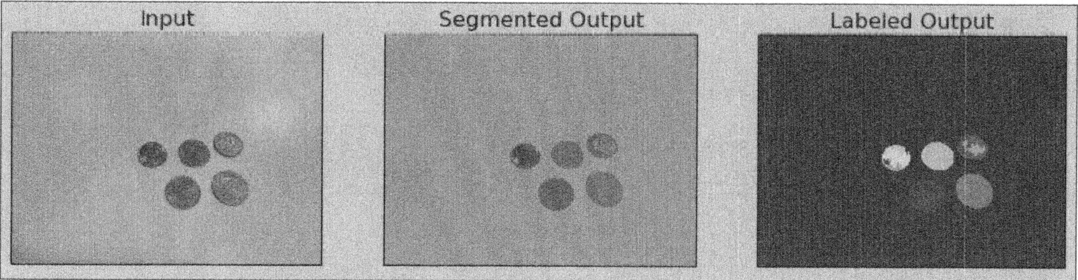

As an exercise, try changing the value of the parameters and compare the different outputs.

K-means clustering and image quantization

The k-means clustering algorithm is a quantization algorithm that maps sets of values within a range into a cluster determined by a value (mean). It basically divides a given set of n values into k partitions. This is called clustering when it's applied on data with two or more dimensions. OpenCV has `cv2.kmeans()` for the implementation of the k-means algorithm. It accepts the following parameters:

- **Data**: This is the data that has to be clustered. If we provide an image, the output will be a quantized (segmented) image. This has to be in the float format.

- **K**: This is the number of partitions in the output set (it is the number of colors in the output if the input is an image).
- **Criteria**: This is the algorithm termination criteria that includes a number of iterations and/or the desired accuracy.
- **Attempts**: This is the number of times the algorithms will be executed using a different initial labeling.
- **Flags**: These specify the initial centers of the clusters, which can have any of the following values:

  ```
  cv2.KMEANS_RANDOM_CENTERS
  cv2.KMEANS_PP_CENTERS
  cv2.KMEANS_USE_INITIAL_LABELS
  ```

The following code is an example of the application of the k-means clustering algorithm on an image with *k* sizes as 2, 4, and 8:

```
import cv2
import numpy as np
import matplotlib.pyplot as plt

image=cv2.imread('/home/pi/book/test_set/4.2.05.tiff')
input = cv2.cvtColor(image,cv2.COLOR_BGR2RGB)

Z=input.reshape((-1,3))
Z=np.float32(Z)

criteria=(cv2.TERM_CRITERIA_EPS+ cv2.TERM_CRITERIA_MAX_ITER,10,1.0)

K=2
ret,label1,center1=cv2.kmeans(Z,K,criteria,10,cv2.KMEANS_RANDOM_
CENTERS)
center1=np.uint8(center1)
res1=center1[label1.flatten()]
output1=res1.reshape((image.shape))

K=4
ret,label2,center2=cv2.kmeans(Z,K,criteria,10,cv2.KMEANS_RANDOM_
CENTERS)
center2=np.uint8(center2)
res2=center2[label2.flatten()]
output2=res2.reshape((image.shape))

K=8
ret,label3,center3=cv2.kmeans(Z,K,criteria,10,cv2.KMEANS_RANDOM_
CENTERS)
```

```
center3=np.uint8(center3)
res3=center3[label3.flatten()]
output3=res3.reshape((image.shape))

titles=['Original','K=2','K=4','K=8']
output=[input,output1,output2,output3]

for i in xrange(4):
  plt.subplot(2,2,i+1),plt.imshow(output[i]),plt.title(titles[i])
  plt.xticks([]),plt.yticks([])
plt.show()
```

We initially assigned random centers to all the clusters with the `cv2.KMEANS_RANDOM_CENTERS` flag. The output of the preceding program will be the original image with the quantized and segmented images, with 2, 4, and 8 colors, as follows:

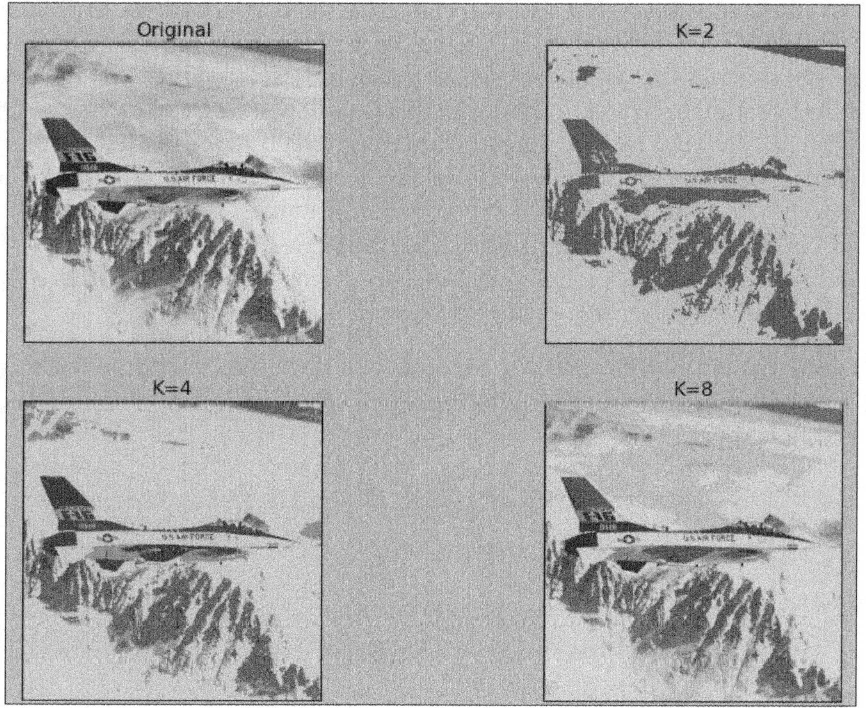

As an exercise, try using the algorithm with different sets and combinations of inputs and compare the results.

Comparison of mean shift and k-means

The k-means algorithm runs *O(n)*, while the mean shift algorithm runs *O(n^2)*. This time, the complexity difference is mainly due to the fact that the k-means algorithm already knows the number of clusters (which is provided when the method is called). However, the mean shift has to come up with the number of clusters itself. In applications where the number of clusters is not known, it is better to use the mean shift algorithm. However, when we do know in advance the number of clusters, it is better to use the k-means algorithm since it runs faster.

Disparity map and depth estimation

Disparity refers to the difference in the location of an object in the corresponding two (left and right) images as seen by the left and right eye, which is created due to a parallax. Our brain uses this disparity to estimate the depth information from the pair of two-dimensional images. We can calculate the disparity between the two images by applying this principle to every pixel in the pair of images. Once we have the disparity information, we can leverage it to estimate the depth just the way our brain uses it to estimate depth. In biology, this is called stereoscopic vision. OpenCV provides the `cv2.StereoBM.compute()` function, which takes the left image and the right image as a parameter and returns the disparity map of the image pair. The `cv2.StereoBM()` function is the constructor that initializes the stereo state. It accepts a preset, the number of disparities (which is a multiple of 16), and `SADWindowSize`, which is a linear block size for comparison. This stereo state is implicitly used to compute disparity map by `cv2.StereoBM.compute()`.

The following program demonstrates the usage of both the functions. For this, you will need two images corresponding to the input from the left camera and the input from the right camera:

```
import cv2
import numpy as np
import matplotlib.pyplot as plt

Right= cv2.imread('/home/pi/book/test_set/tsukuba-r.tif',0)
Left = cv2.imread('/home/pi/book/test_set/tsukuba-l.tif',0)

stereo_BM_state=cv2.StereoBM(preset=cv2.STEREO_BM_BASIC_PRESET,ndispar
ities=32,SADWindowSize=27)
output_map=stereo_BM_state.compute(Left,Right)

titles=['Left','Right','Depth Map']
output=[Left,Right,output_map]
```

```
for i in xrange(3):
  plt.subplot(1,3,i+1),plt.imshow(output[i],cmap='gray'),
  plt.title(titles[i])
  plt.xticks([]),plt.yticks([])
plt.show()
```

The output will be as follows:

A smaller `SADWindowSize` value will provide a detailed but distorted map, and a higher value will provide a smoother map, as seen in the preceding output. As an exercise, try out different values of `ndisparities` and `SADWindowSize`. `SADWindowSize` has to be an odd positive value.

In the preceding image, the brighter areas denote more disparity, which means that the objects in the input images corresponding to the brighter areas in the output image are closer to the cameras. In the same way, the darker colors in the disparity map mean that the corresponding objects in the images are farther from the camera.

Summary

In this chapter, we explored the concepts of image inpainting, segmentation, and depth estimation.

In the next chapter, we will learn and implement a few more advanced concepts such as histograms, contours, and morphological operators.

8
Histograms, Contours, Morphological Transformations, and Performance Measurement

Having learned the basics and intermediate topics of computer vision and image processing, we will now move on to the more advanced topics with this chapter, which will also prepare us for the next chapter on real-life applications. We will explore the following topics in this chapter:

- Image histograms
- Contours in an image
- Morphological transformations on an image
- The performance measurement of OpenCV

Image histograms

A histogram is a way to graphically represent the distribution of data. An image histogram is the representation of an image array. It represents the tonal distribution of the digital image. Basically, the histogram of an image is a graphical representation of the distribution of color or luminance variance in an image. In an image histogram, the *x* axis represents the variation of colors, and the *y* axis represents the total number of pixels for a particular color tone. If we were to plot a histogram for a grayscale image, the *x* axis will represent the different intensity values (0 to 255, for example), and the *y* axis will represent the number of pixels that have such values.

In a similar way, we can plot the histogram for color images by plotting the image histogram for each channel (red, green, and blue, for example).

Let's get started by plotting a histogram of a grayscale image. We will use the `hist()` function that belongs to the matplotlib library. Run the following code:

```
import cv2
import matplotlib.pyplot as plt

img = cv2.imread('/home/pi/book/test_set/4.1.08.tiff',0)
plt.hist(img.ravel(),256,[0,256])
plt.show()
```

In the preceding code, we passed an image, the number of vertical edges in the histogram, and a range as an argument to the `plt.hist()` function. You can pass more arguments to this function.

See the documentation of this function for more information here: `http://matplotlib.org/api/pyplot_api.html`

The output of the preceding code is as follows:

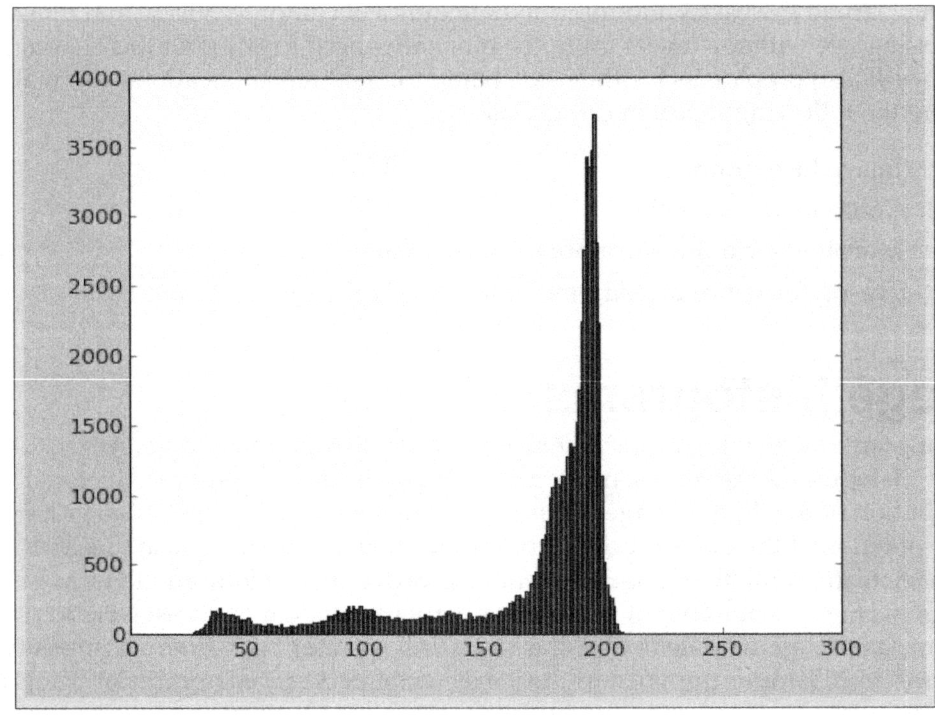

OpenCV also has a function to plot histograms for color images. The `cv2.calcHist()` function accepts an image, channel, mask, size, and range as arguments. The following example shows its usage by plotting a histogram for each channel (red, green, and blue):

```
import cv2
from matplotlib import pyplot as plt

img = cv2.imread('/home/pi/book/test_set/4.2.03.tiff',1)

input=cv2.cvtColor(img,cv2.COLOR_RGB2BGR)
histr_RED = cv2.calcHist([input],[0],None,[256],[0,256])
histr_GREEN = cv2.calcHist([input],[1],None,[256],[0,256])
histr_BLUE = cv2.calcHist([input],[2],None,[256],[0,256])

plt.subplot(221),plt.imshow(input),plt.title('Original
  Image'),plt.xticks([]),plt.yticks([])
plt.subplot(222),plt.plot(histr_RED,color='r'),
  plt.title('Red'), plt.xlim([0,256]), plt.yticks([])
plt.subplot(223),plt.plot(histr_GREEN,color='g'), plt.title('Green'),
plt.xlim([0,256]), plt.yticks([])
plt.subplot(224),plt.plot(histr_BLUE,color='b'), plt.title('Blue'),
plt.xlim([0,256]), plt.yticks([])
plt.show()
```

The following is the output of the code. You can enable the display of the values on the y axis by omitting the `plt.yticks([])` code for the `plt.plot()` statement:

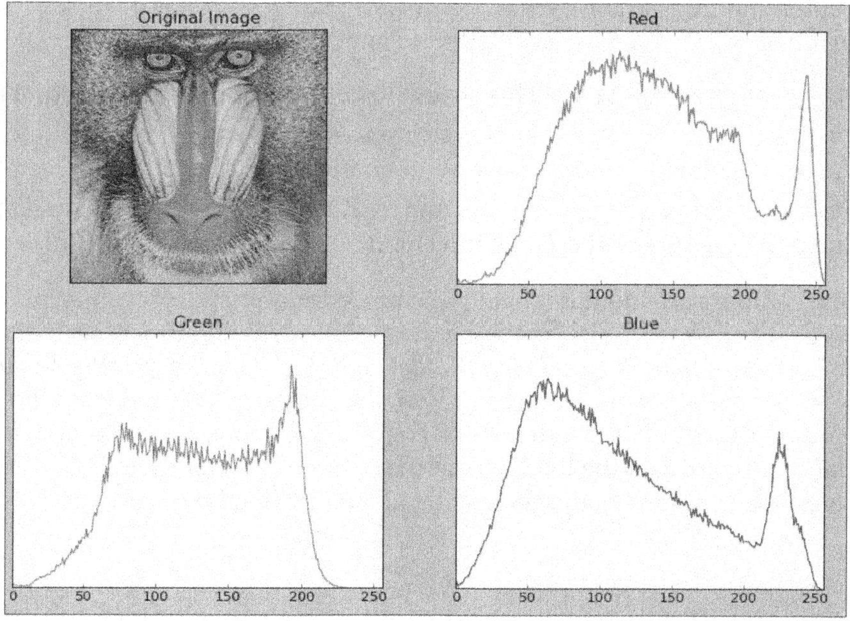

The NumPy library also has an `np.histogram()` histogram function that can be used to plot the histogram of an image. Check the details of this function and implement a program to plot a histogram as an exercise for this section.

You can refer to `http://docs.scipy.org/doc/numpy/reference/generated/numpy.histogram.html` for more details for this exercise.

Image contours

A contour is a curve joining all the continuous points along the boundary with the same color value. The detecting of contours in an image is very useful if you want to detect the boundaries in images. In an image, the edges are computed as points that are the extremes of the image gradient in the direction of the gradient. Contours are often obtained from edges, but they are aimed to be object contours. Thus, they need to be closed curves and are different from edges.

It is helpful to threshold an image before extracting contours to increase the accuracy of the image.

OpenCV has `cv2.findContours()` to find the contours in an image. It takes an image, a contour retrieval mode, and a contour approximation method as arguments and returns the contours of the image. Contour retrieval mode can be `CV_RETR_EXTERNAL`, `CV_RETR_LIST`, `CV_RETR_CCOMP`, or `CV_RETR_TREE`. The contour approximation method can be `CV_CHAIN_APPROX_NONE`, `CV_CHAIN_APPROX_SIMPLE`, `CV_CHAIN_APPROX_TC89_L1`, or `CV_CHAIN_APPROX_TC89_KCOS`.

- `CV_CHAIN_APPROX_NONE`: This stores absolutely all the contour points
- `CV_CHAIN_APPROX_SIMPLE`: This compresses horizontal, vertical, and diagonal segments and leaves only their end points
- `CV_CHAIN_APPROX_TC89_L1`, `CV_CHAIN_APPROX_TC89_KCOS`: These apply to one of the flavors of the Teh-Chin chain approximation algorithm

Once all the contours are identified using the preceding function, it can be plotted using `cv2.drawContours()`. It works like most of the drawing functions that we saw in *Chapter 2, Working with Images, Webcams, and GUI*. The function takes as arguments the image where the contours are to be drawn, the contours detected from the `cv2.findContours()` function, the index of the contour to be drawn (`-1` for drawing all of them), and the color and the thickness of the contour. The following code identifies and draws all the contours in an image with a blue line that has a thickness of 2:

```
import cv2
import matplotlib.pyplot as plt
```

```
img = cv2.imread('/home/pi/book/test_set/4.2.07.tiff')
input = cv2.cvtColor(img,cv2.COLOR_BGR2RGB)
gray = cv2.cvtColor(img,cv2.COLOR_BGR2GRAY)
ret,thresh = cv2.threshold(gray,127,255,0)
contours, hierarchy = cv2.findContours(
  thresh,cv2.RETR_TREE,cv2.CHAIN_APPROX_SIMPLE)

cv2.drawContours(input, contours, -1, (0,0,255), 2)

plt.imshow(input),plt.title('Contours')
plt.xticks([]),plt.yticks([])
plt.show()
```

In the preceding code, `cv2.drawContours(input, contours, -1, (0,0,255), 2)` is used to draw all the contours. If you need to draw a specific contour, then you can use a function such as `cv2.drawContours(input, contours, 2, (0,0,255), 2)` by specifying the contour index.

The output of the preceding code is as follows:

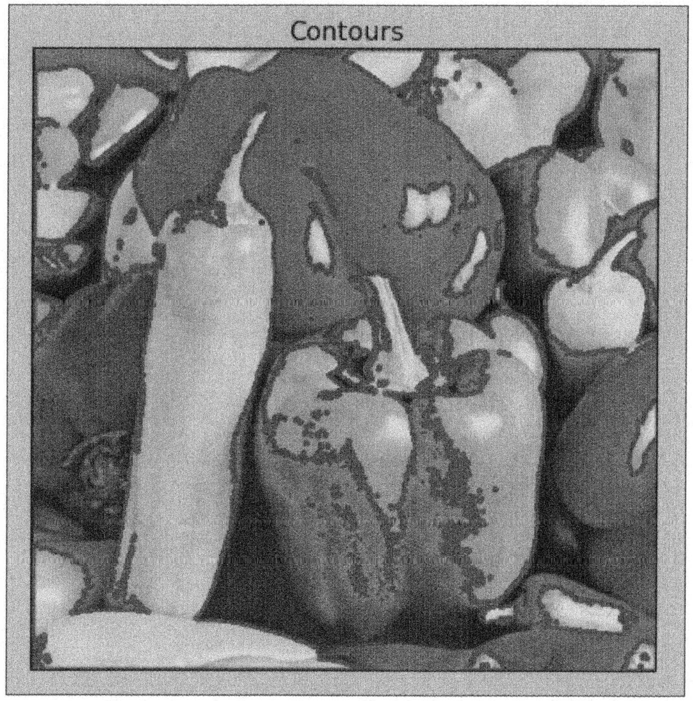

As an exercise to this section, try to use `cv2.findContours()` with different combinations of method and mode and compare the output.

Morphological transformations on image

Morphological operations are based on the shape of an image, and they work best on binary images. We can use these to do away with a lot of unwanted information, such as noise in an image. Any morphological operation requires two inputs—an image and a kernel. In this section, we will explore the erosion, dilation, and gradient of an image. Since binary images are the most suitable for the explanation of this concept, we will use a binary image (black and white) to study the concepts.

Erosion removes the boundaries in an image and slims it. In a binary image, white is the foreground and black is the background. All the pixels at the boundary of the white foreground image are made zero, thus slimming the image and eroding away the boundary. Dilation is exactly the opposite of erosion. It expands the foreground image boundary and flattens it. The extent of erosion and dilation depends on the kernel and the number of iterations. The morphological gradient of an image is the difference between the dilatation and erosion. It will return the outline of an image. Check out the following code for the basic usage of these operations in OpenCV. We will use these in our next chapter to refine our image for a better output:

```
import numpy as np
import cv2
from matplotlib import pyplot as plt

img = cv2.imread('/home/pi/book/test_set/morphological.tif',0)
kernel = np.ones((5,5),np.uint8)
erosion = cv2.erode(img,kernel,iterations = 2)
dilation = cv2.dilate(img,kernel,iterations = 2)
gradient = cv2.morphologyEx(img, cv2.MORPH_GRADIENT, kernel)

titles=['Original','Erosion','Dilation','Gradient']
output=[img,erosion,dilation,gradient]

for i in xrange(4):
  plt.subplot(2,2,i+1),plt.imshow(output[i],cmap='gray')
  plt.title(titles[i]),plt.xticks([]),plt.yticks([])
plt.show()
```

The output will be as follows:

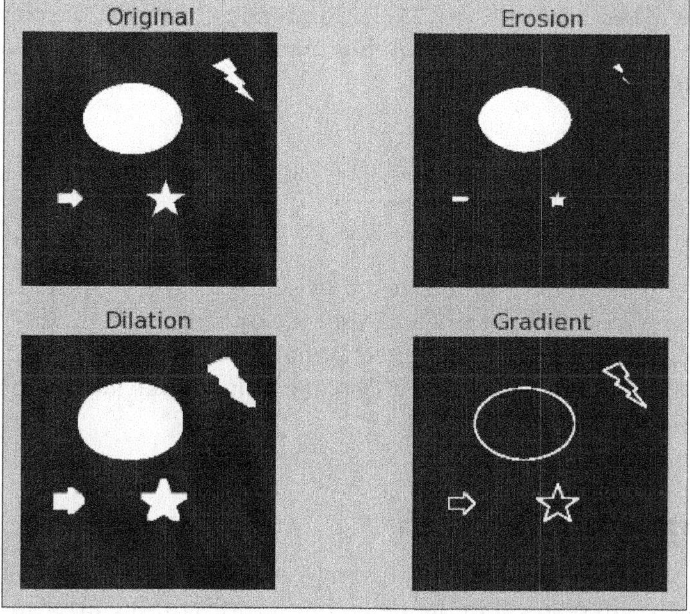

In our example, we created the 5x5 kernel of all the images and applied it to the image. OpenCV provides the `cv2.getStructuringElement()` function that returns a kernel with the given shape and size. The size is an odd positive integer and the shape can be one of `cv2.MORPH_RECT`, `cv2.MORPH_ELLIPSE`, or `cv2.MORPH_CROSS`.

As an exercise to this section, apply the custom kernels on the image for morphological operations.

OpenCV performance measurement and improvement

In Python, we can use the time library to obtain the current time. This allows us to measure how long a piece of code takes to run, as shown in the following code:

```
t1 = time.time()
# Image Processing code goes here
t2 = time.time()
print (t2-t1)
```

OpenCV also provides `cv2.getTickCount()` and `cv2.getTickFrequency()`, which can be used for the same purpose. The `cv2.getTickCount()` function returns the number of clock cycles and `cv2.getTickFrequency()` returns the clock frequency. We can use these functions in the following manner to get the time required to execute the code:

```
c1=cv2.getTickCount()
# Image processing code goes here
c2=cv2.getTickCount()
print ((c2-c1)/cv2.getTickFrequency())
```

We can optimize the OpenCV functions by using `cv2.setUseOptimized()`, which accepts a Boolean value as a parameter to set the optimization mode. It's set to true by default after installation. You can check whether the optimization is enabled with `cv2.useOptimized()`, which returns a Boolean value (`True` stands for enabled, and `False` for disabled).

Summary

In this chapter, we covered histograms, image contours, and morphological operations, which will be used in the next chapter for real-life applications.

Our next chapter will be a culmination of the image processing techniques that we have learned and explored so far. We will build some real-life applications, such as a movement detector, green screen effect, gesture recognition, and barcode detection in images.

9
Real-life Computer Vision Applications

Until now, we have studied a wide variety of concepts in computer vision and their implementations in OpenCV. Now it's time to build some real-life applications. In this chapter, we will implement the following basic applications:

- Barcode detection
- Motion detection and tracking
- Hand gesture detection
- Chroma key with green screen in the live video

Barcode detection

A barcode is a machine-readable 2D image (data) format. It is usually used to store information about a product. Originally, a barcode was represented by parallel lines of varying width and separated by spaces. Later, it evolved into multiple formats.

In this section, we will see how to detect a single basic parallel line barcode from an image. What follows is an example of an image with a barcode:

Let's read the image using the following code:

```
import numpy as np
import cv2

image=cv2.imread('/home/pi/book/test_set/test5.png',1)
input = cv2.cvtColor(image, cv2.COLOR_BGR2GRAY)
```

A barcode always has a very high horizontal gradient and a very low vertical gradient. So, in our image, we need to search for a region that fulfills this property. The best way to accomplish this is to compute the Sobel derivatives of the first order in horizontal and vertical directions, and then subtract the vertical derivative from the horizontal derivative:

```
hor_der = cv2.Sobel(input, ddepth = -1 , dx = 1, dy = 0,
  ksize = 5)
ver_der = cv2.Sobel(input, ddepth = -1 , dx = 0, dy = 1,
  ksize = 5)

diff = cv2.subtract(hor_der, ver_der)
```

Then, we need to convert the output in 8-bit unsigned integer format using this code:

```
diff = cv2.convertScaleAbs(diff)
```

This will yield the following image:

This output highlights the regions that have a high gradient in the horizontal direction and a low gradient in the vertical direction. We can apply Gaussian blur to this using the following code:

```
blur = cv2.GaussianBlur(diff, (3, 3),0)
```

The output of this is a blurred and smoothened image, as seen here:

Then, we will apply a binary threshold to this blurred image with 255 as the threshold value, with the following code:

```
ret, th = cv2.threshold(blur, 225, 255, cv2.THRESH_BINARY)
```

This will yield a binary image, as follows:

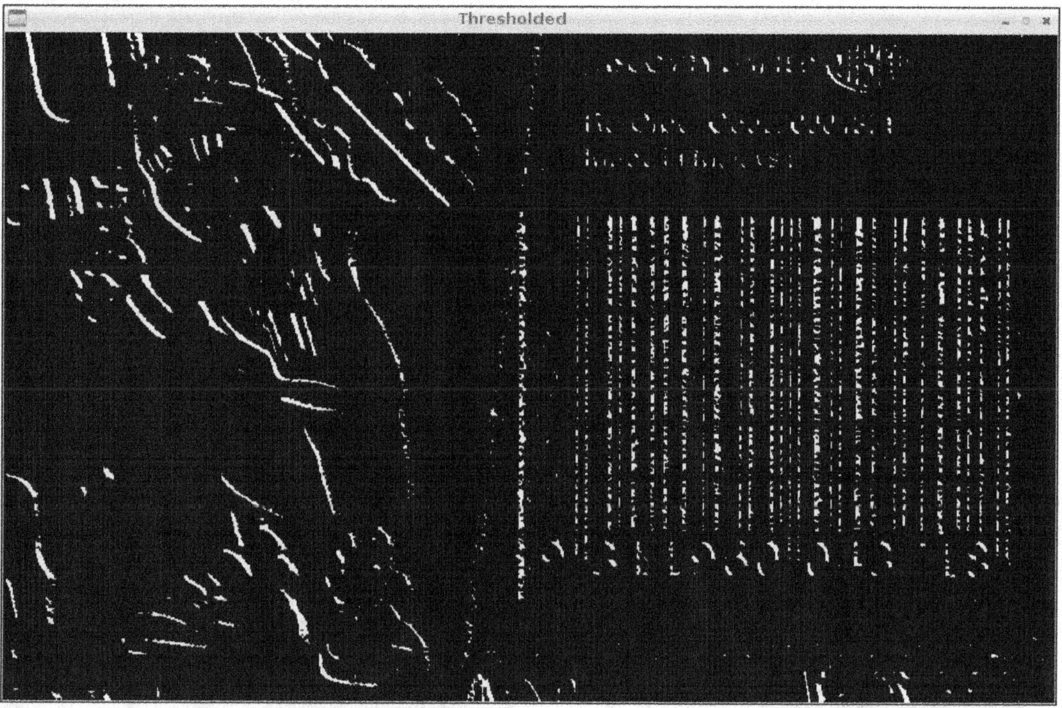

Now, we have the binary image of a barcode in this output. We can fill in the gaps between the bars of the barcode by dilating it:

```
dilated = cv2.dilate(th, None, iterations = 10)
```

The output will contain a big rectangle-like box corresponding to the barcode region in the original image with some other white regions that we are not interested in.

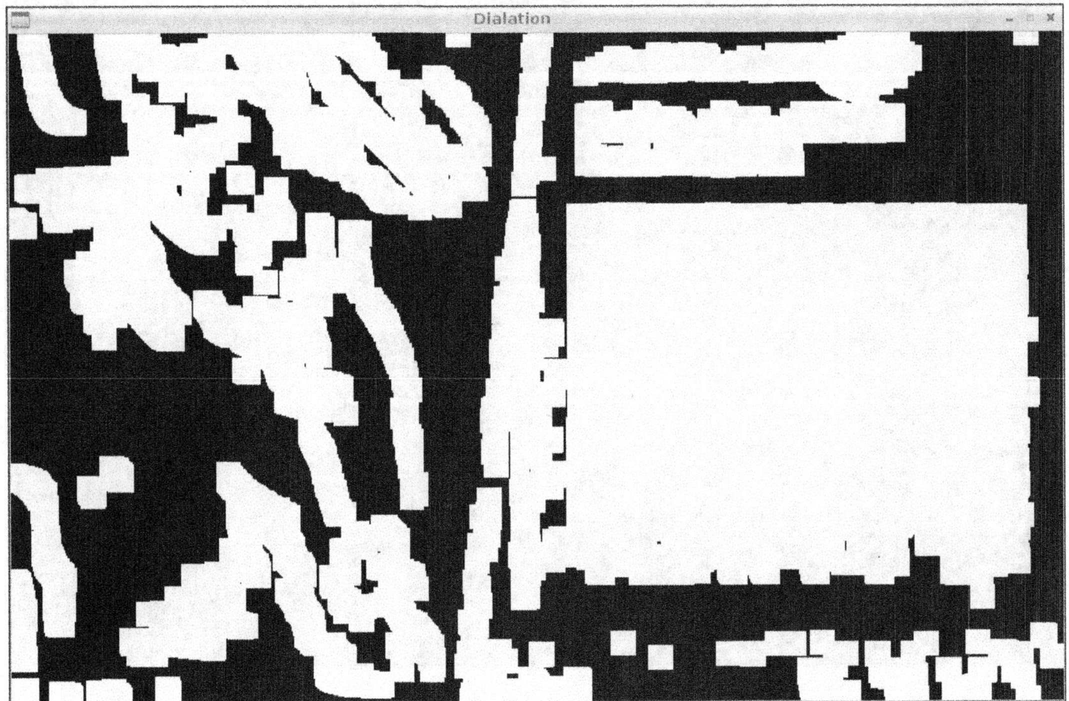

We can eliminate the other region that we're not interested in with the erosion operation:

```
eroded = cv2.erode(dilated, None, iterations = 15)
```

This will eliminate most of the unwanted white regions and will also shrink the white rectangle-like region which corresponds to the barcode.

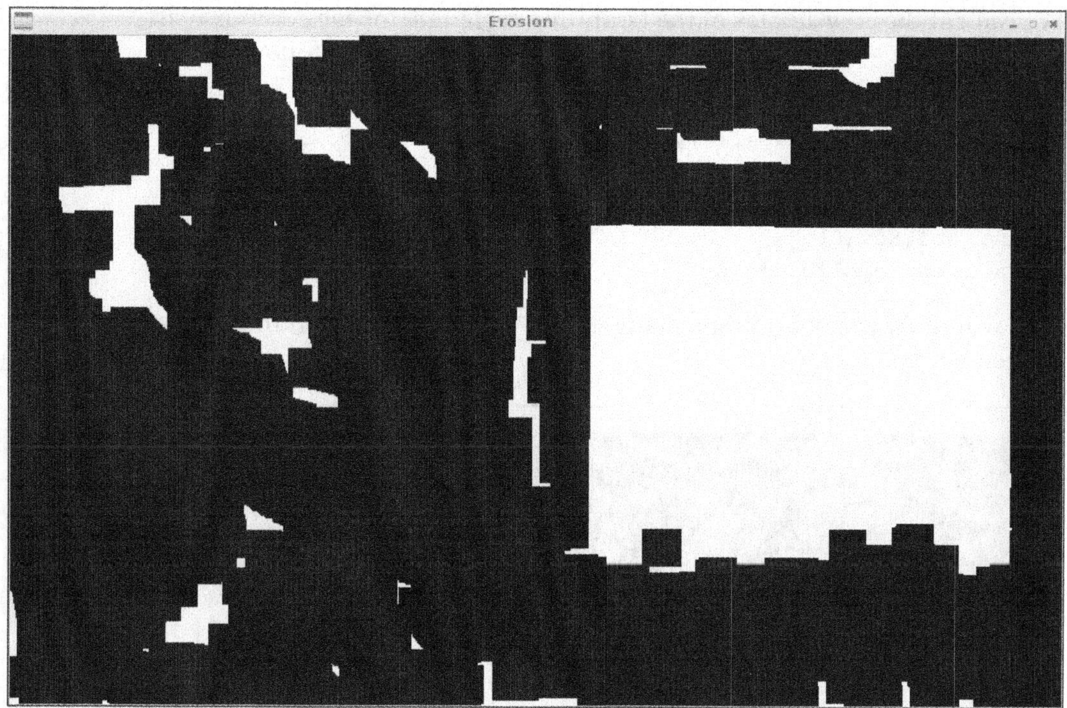

The next task is very simple. We can find out the list of contours in this binary image with the following code:

```
(contours, hierarchy) = cv2.findContours(eroded,
  cv2.RETR_TREE,cv2.CHAIN_APPROX_SIMPLE)
```

The biggest contour in this image would be the contour corresponding to the barcode region. We can find out the biggest contour with this code:

```
areas = [cv2.contourArea(temp) for temp in contours]
max_index = np.argmax(areas)
largest_contour=contours[max_index]
```

We can get the coordinates of the bounding rectangle for the contour with `cv2.boundingRect()`, an OpenCV function, and draw it as follows:

```
x,y,width,height = cv2.boundingRect(largest_contour)
cv2.rectangle(image,(x,y),(x+width,y+height),(0,255,0),2)

cv2.imshow('Detected Barcode',image)
cv2.waitKey(0)
cv2.destroyAllWindows()
```

This will draw the bounding rectangle over the area corresponding to the barcode, as seen here:

In this manner, we have detected the barcode in the image. Now, this code may not work for all sample images, and you might want to alter the values of the parameters with the following lines of code to suit your sample:

```
blur = cv2.GaussianBlur(diff, (3, 3),0)
```

You can also use other blurring functions and adjust the kernel to suit your sample.

Furthermore, in the dilation and erosion operation, you can play with a number of iterations:

```
dilated = cv2.dilate(th, None, iterations = 10)
eroded = cv2.erode(dilated, None, iterations = 15)
```

You might want to extend this program to build a live webcam barcode detector. Our next real-life applications will be based on live videos and we will use a webcam to capture live videos.

Motion detection and tracking

We will now build a sophisticated motion detection and tracking system with a very simple logic of finding the difference between subsequent frames from a video feed, like a webcam stream, and plotting contours around the area where the difference is detected.

Let's import the required libraries and initialize the webcam:

```
import cv2
import numpy as np

cap = cv2.VideoCapture(0)
```

We will need a kernel for the dilation operation, which we will create in advance, rather than creating it every time in the loop:

```
k=np.ones((3,3),np.uint8)
```

The following code will capture and store subsequent frames:

```
t0 = cap.read()[1]
t1 = cap.read()[1]
```

Now, we will initiate the while loop and calculate the difference between both frames, and then convert the output to grayscale for further processing:

```
whilc(Truc):

    d=cv2.absdiff(t1,t0)

    grey = cv2.cvtColor(d, cv2.COLOR_BGR2GRAY)
```

The output will be as follows, showing the difference of pixels between the frames:

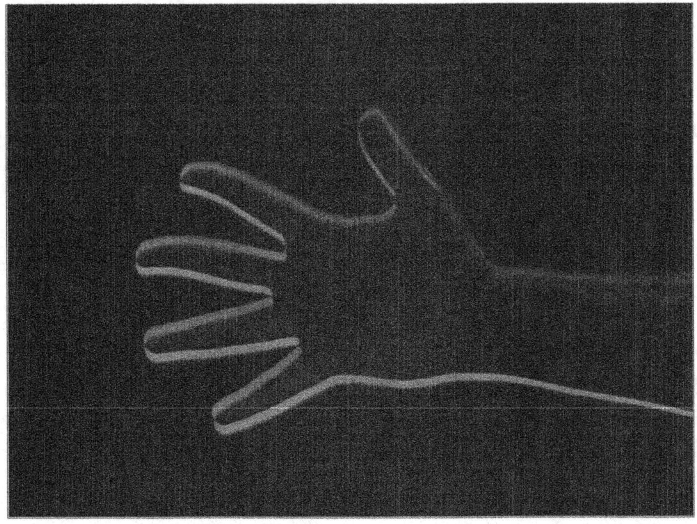

This image may contain some noise, so we will blur it first:

```
blur = cv2.GaussianBlur(grey,(3,3),0)
```

We use the binary threshold to convert this noise-removed output into a binary image with the following code:

```
ret, th = cv2.threshold( blur, 15, 255, cv2.THRESH_BINARY )
```

The final operation is to dilate the image so that it is easier for us to find the boundary clearly:

```
dilated=cv2.dilate(th,k,iterations=2)
```

The output of the preceding step is the following:

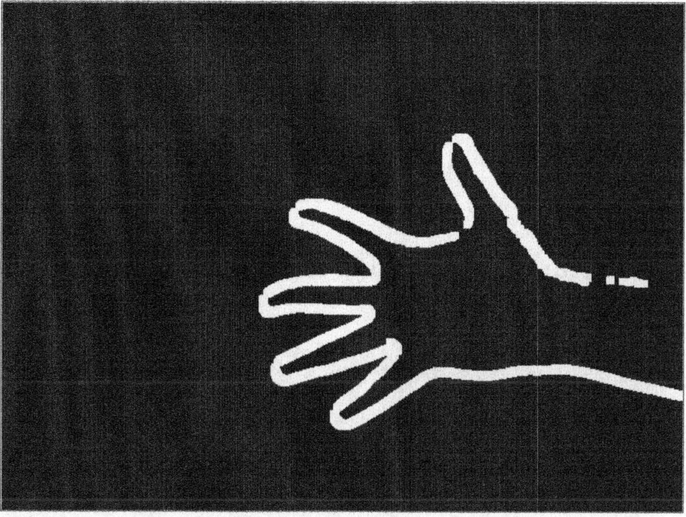

Then, we will find and draw the contours for the preceding image with the following code:

```
contours, hierarchy = cv2.findContours(
  dilated,cv2.RETR_TREE,cv2.CHAIN_APPROX_SIMPLE)

t2=t0
cv2.drawContours(t2, contours, -1, (0,255,0), 2 )

cv2.imshow('Output', t2 )
```

Finally, we will assign the latest frame to the older frame and capture the next frame with a webcam:

```
t0=t1
t1=cap.read()[1]
```

We will terminate the loop once we detect the *Esc* keypress, as usual:

```
        if cv2.waitKey(5) == 27 :
            break
```

Once the loop is terminated, we will release the camera and destroy the display window:

```
    cap.release()
    cv2.destroyAllWindows()
```

This will draw the contour roughly around the area where the movement is detected, as seen in the following image:

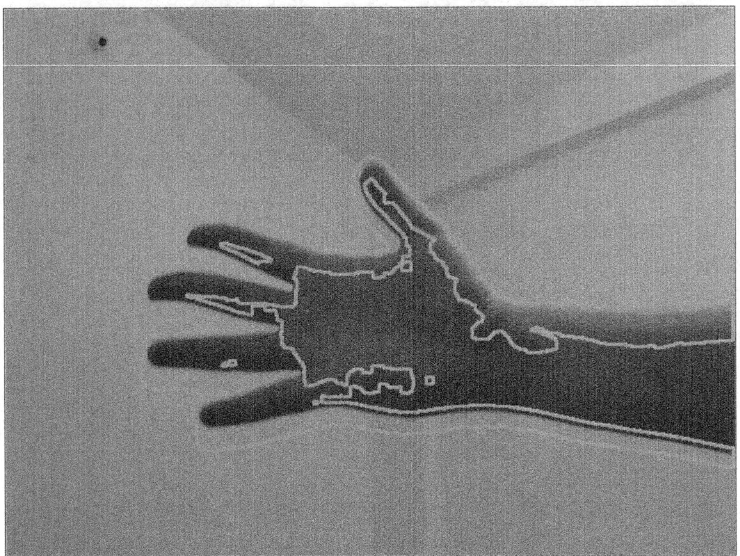

This code works very well for slow movements. You can make the output more interesting by drawing contours with different colors. Also, you can find out the centroid of the contours and draw crosshairs or circles corresponding to the centroids.

Hand gesture recognition

Gesture recognition denotes the interpretation of human gestures by a computer to perform a specific task. Gesture recognition systems try to interpret the gestures originating from hands, faces, body posture, or movements of the eye. Gesture recognition can employ one of the wide varieties of specialized input devices, such as gloves, depth stereo cameras, or body sensors. However, the simplest form of gesture recognition can be implemented using a simple camera as an input device (for example, our webcam). We are going to implement code to count the number of fingers in the hand held in front of the camera. This application will make use of the concept of convex hull, which we will see when coding.

Let's get started with importing the libraries and reading the frame:

```
import numpy as np
import cv2

cap = cv2.VideoCapture(0)

while( True ) :
ret , frame = cap.read()
```

Once we capture the frame, let's convert it to grayscale and remove the noise by blurring it:

```
    gray=cv2.cvtColor(frame,cv2.COLOR_BGR2GRAY)

    blur=cv2.GaussianBlur(gray,(3,3),0)
```

The output will be as follows, containing a hand with some background:

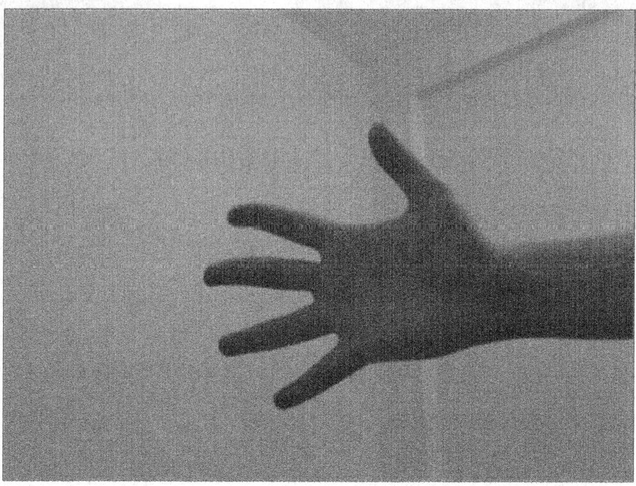

Now, the next task is to extract the area of the hand from the background, so that we could use it to recognize gestures. The best way to achieve this is to segment the image by binarizing it. We can use the thresholding mechanism to achieve this. However, if we use simple binary thresholding, then we need to adjust the threshold parameter every time there is a change in background. If you recall *Chapter 4, Colorspaces, Transformations, and Thresholds*, we have already explored Otsu's method, which is suitable for an image that is bimodal (an image that has an object and a background). Our captured grayscale image fits this model very well, so we will use Otsu's method to binarize the image. The method will work fine as long as the background color is not the same as the color of the skin:

```
ret , th = cv2.threshold(
  blur,0,255,cv2.THRESH_BINARY_INV+cv2.THRESH_OTSU)
```

This will result in a binary image with hand pixels as white and background as black, as seen in the following image:

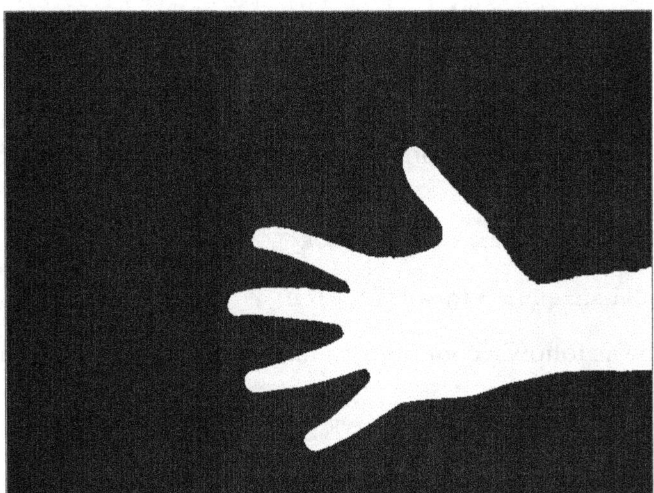

This really makes it easy for us to find the contours in the image:

```
(contours, hierarchy) = cv2.findContours(th,
  cv2.RETR_TREE,cv2.CHAIN_APPROX_SIMPLE)
```

As we have seen in the last two applications, the following code will find the largest contour; in case there are multiple contours, due to other objects in the background, the largest contour will always be the hand, as it is relatively nearer to the camera:

```
areas = [cv2.contourArea(temp) for temp in contours]
max_index = np.argmax(areas)
largest_contour=contours[max_index]
```

You might want to draw the intermediate output `largest_contour` on the image for better understanding. This output would be a polygon curve with many vertices, which will not be very useful for our application. We can approximate it with the use of `cv2.approxPolyDP()` to a polygon with fewer vertices. This function uses the Douglas-Peucker algorithm. This line of code does the trick:

```
approx=cv2.approxPolyDP(largest_contour,
  0.01*cv2.arcLength(largest_contour,True),True)
```

Again, you might want to draw the `approx` value on the original image and compare it with the shape of the hand.

We are done with most of the difficult parts in the logic, and the remainder is straightforward. The last step before we use this input for gesture recognition is to determine the convex hull of this polygon.

Let's try to understand the idea of convex hull in the simplest way. Imagine a plain board hammered with a few nails on it. If we try to put an elastic band around it, it will stretch and create a convex shape, which is nothing but the convex hull of all the nails hammered into the plain board.

For our application, we will use the vertices of the approximated polygon contour of the hand to determine the convex hull:

```
hull = cv2.convexHull(approx,returnPoints=True)
```

This will return a set of points that can be used to draw the convex hull of the hand boundary. We can use `len(hull)` to determine the number of fingers in the hand held before the camera:

```
cv2.putText(frame,'Number of Fingers ' + str (len(hull)-2),
  (10,30),cv2.FONT_HERSHEY_COMPLEX_SMALL,1,(255,0,0))
```

The following code draws the convex hull around the hand:

```
cv2.drawContours(frame,[hull],0,(0,0,255),1)
```

And the following code draws concentric circles around the vertices of the convex hull:

```
for i in range ( len ( hull ) ):
  [x , y]= hull[i][0].flatten()
  cv2.circle(frame,(int(x),int(y)),2,(0,255,0),-1)
  cv2.circle(frame,(int(x),int(y)),5,(255,255,0),1)
  cv2.circle(frame,(int(x),int(y)),8,(255,0,0),1)
```

```
        print "Number of Fingers " + str ( (len(hull)-2) )
        cv2.imshow('Gestures',frame)

            if cv2.waitKey(5) == 27:
                break

    cv2.destroyAllWindows()
    cap.release()
```

You must have noticed that we are subtracting `2` from the total number of vertices to adjust the two extra vertices that we get at the edge of the image, as follows:

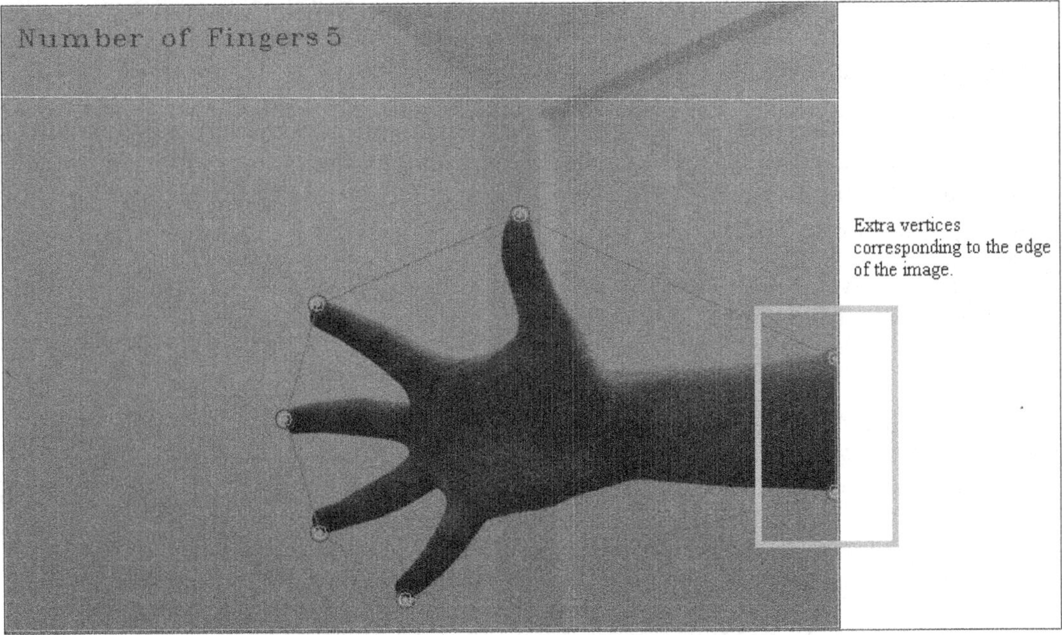

In the preceding example, we have detected five fingers. If we bend a finger, then we will get the following output:

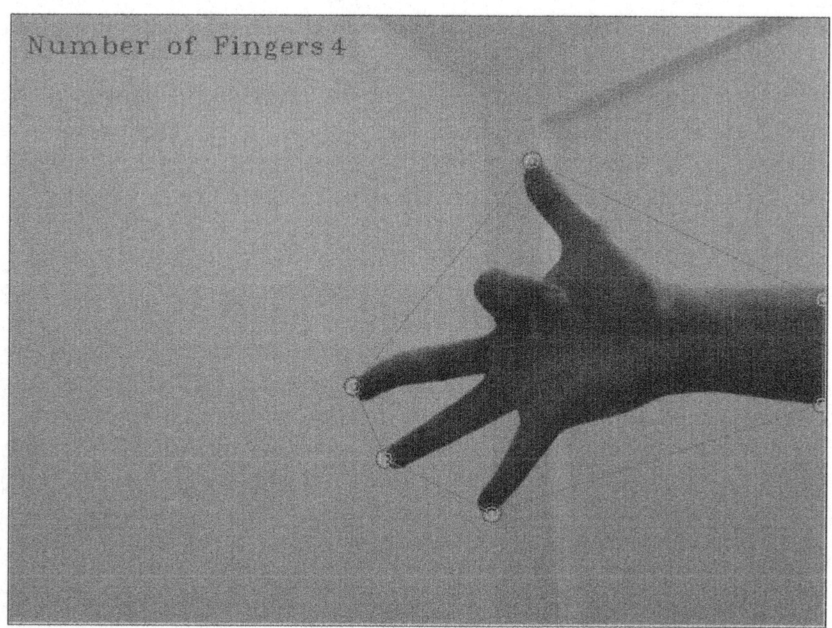

Similarly, if we bend two fingers, then the output would be something like this:

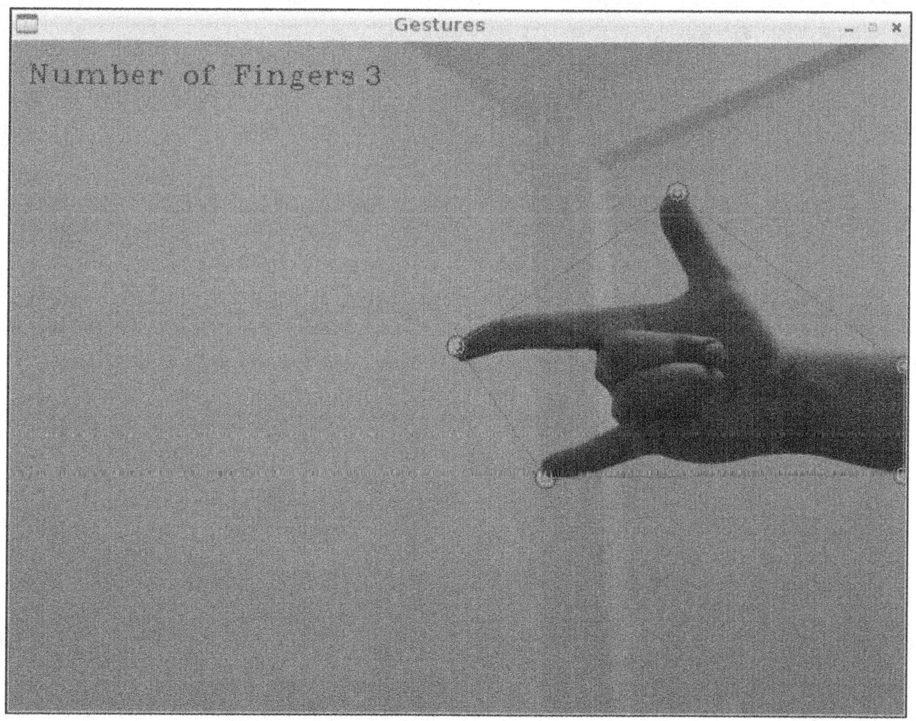

This program does not always guarantee the correct output. For example, for a single finger, it would never show the correct output. This program can be improved by using the concept of convexity defects to count the number of fingers. Once we have determined the number of fingers, we can use that number to perform a variety of operations based on the value of the number. The simplest application would be a hand gesture-based video recording system.

Chroma key with green screen

Chroma key is a special effect and a post-production technique in which multiple images can be combined together. This technique is widely used to replace green or blue backgrounds in an image with another image or live video to create special effects in live action or animation movies and weather forecasting. The logic on which the chroma key technique is based is very simple. We use a uniform-colored background, usually bright green or blue, and then replace that with an image or another live video.

Let's get started by importing the needed packages and by initializing the capture:

```
import numpy as np
import cv2

cam = cv2.VideoCapture(0)
```

For better results, we can set the camera resolution to 640 x 480, as at this resolution we will get a better frame rate:

```
cam.set(3,640)
cam.set(4,480)
```

Next, we read the background image with the same resolution (640 x 480), which is an image of earth from space. The camera resolution and the background image resolution must be the same as all logical and arithmetic functions on the image that we need to use will require all the input images to be of the same resolution:

```
bg = cv2.imread('/home/pi/book/test_set/space.jpg',1)
```

Then, we initialize the loop and read the frames from the camera:

```
while ( True ):
  ret, frame = cam.read()
```

We will use a green cloth or paper for the background and a Raspberry Pi 2 box as the object. The original frame is as follows:

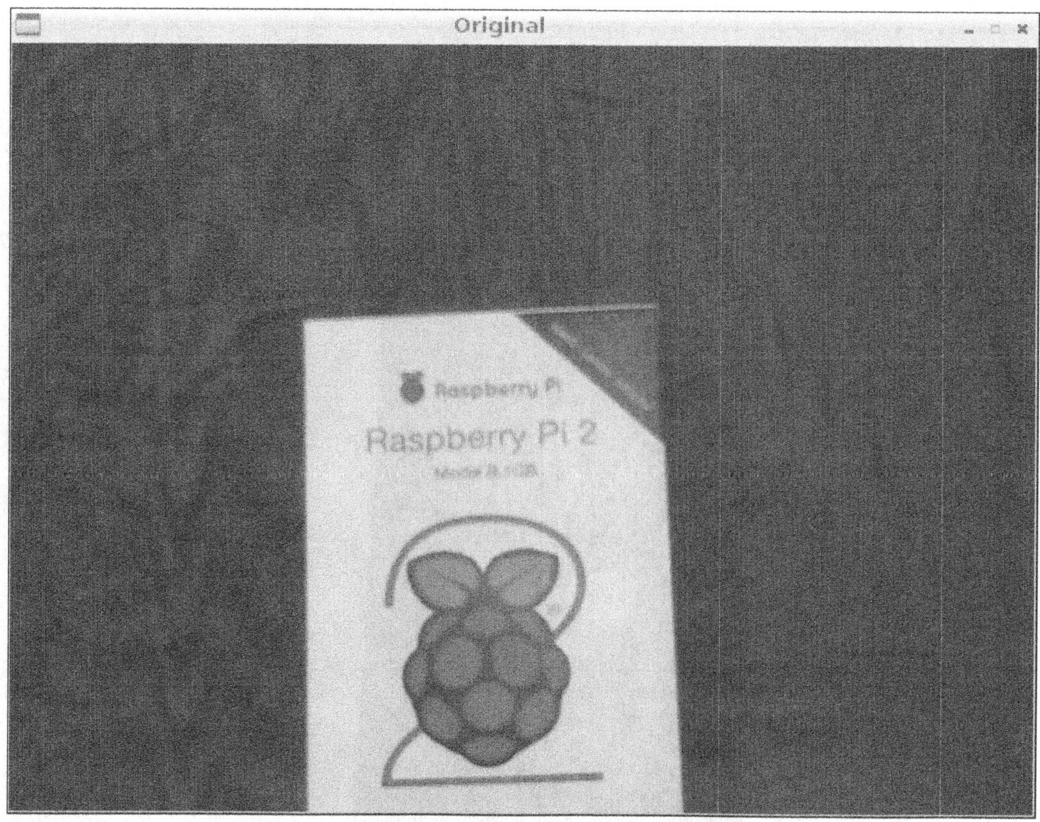

As we have seen in *Chapter 4, Colorspaces, Transformations, and Thresholds*, the HSV color format is the most appropriate format for any type of activity that involves operation on a range of colors; we will convert the image into the HSV format and calculate the mask for the green background, as follows:

```
hsv=cv2.cvtColor(frame,cv2.COLOR_BGR2HSV)

image_mask=cv2.inRange(hsv,np.array([40,50,50]),
  np.array([80,255,255]))
```

The image mask will appear as seen here, where green pixels are replaced by the color white and others are assigned the color black:

Once we have obtained the background image mask, we can easily apply it on the background image to obscure the foreground object with black pixels as follows:

```
bg_mask=cv2.bitwise_and(bg,bg,mask=image_mask)
```

The result will replace all the white pixels with the background image and the foreground area will still have the black pixels, as seen here:

Now, we need to extract only the foreground image from our camera feed. This can be accomplished by using the following code:

```
fg_mask=cv2.bitwise_and(frame,
  frame,mask=cv2.bitwise_not(image_mask))
```

This will extract all the non-green objects, while assigning the color black to the pixels corresponding to the green background.

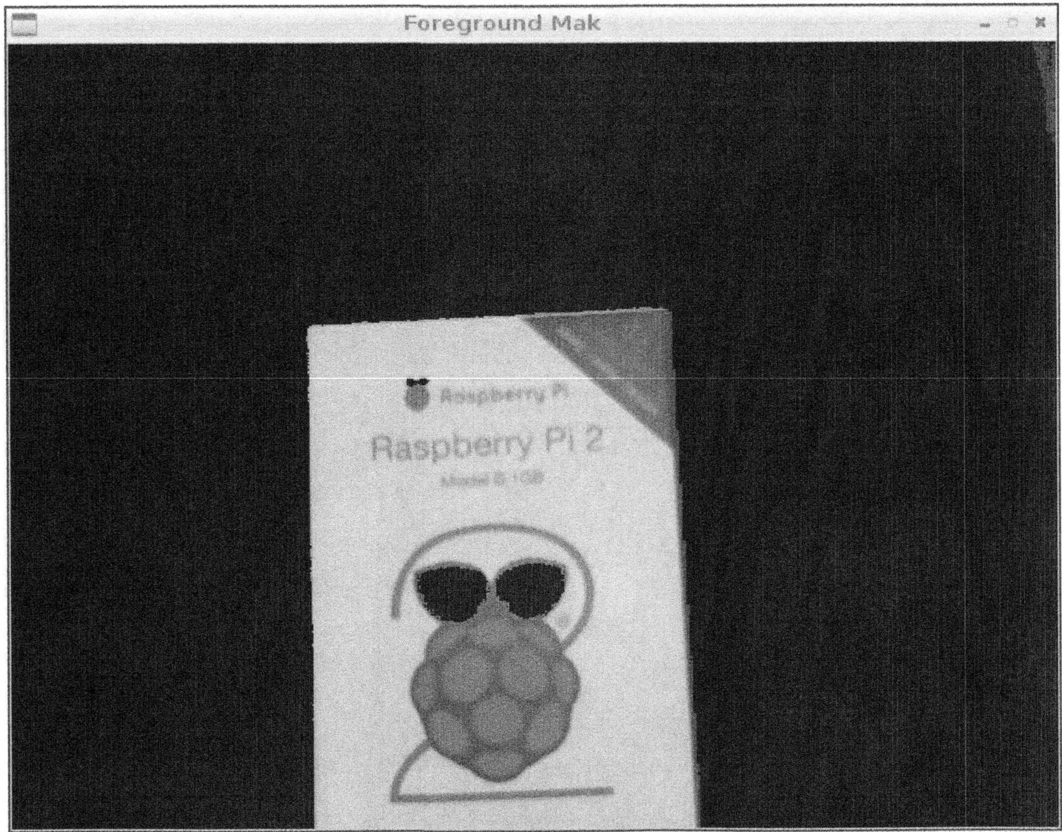

Finally, we will add our last two image outputs, which will provide us with the required chroma key effect, by replacing the green screen with the earth image in space:

```
    cv2.imshow('Output',cv2.add(bg_mask,fg_mask))

     if cv2.waitKey(1) == 27:
     break

cv2.destroyAllWindows()
cam.release()
```

The desired visual effect will appear as follows:

You have achieved a Hollywood-style chroma key effect with a green screen. You must have noticed that in the preceding output, the green leaves in the Raspberry Pi 2 log on the box are also replaced by the background image, as it falls under the color range we specified in the `inRange()` function. You can achieve better results by replacing the green screen with a blue screen and changing the color range from green to blue in the `inRange()` function. The key rule is that the object in the foreground should not have the color of the background screen. So, if you are using a green screen, make sure that the foreground object does not include the color green (the same applies to blue screen too).

Summary

In this chapter, we have seen how to leverage the computer vision techniques we previously studied to implement real-life applications. From here onwards, you can explore OpenCV in more detail and create more real-life applications, which will suit your project requirements by combining various techniques together. In the next chapter, we will explore another powerful, yet simple, computer vision library for Python: SimpleCV, and we will implement the chroma key effect again along with few other real-life applications.

10
Introduction to SimpleCV

We explored image and video processing techniques in OpenCV from chapters 1 to 8. In *Chapter 9, Real-life Computer Vision Applications*, we implemented quite a few real-life applications with OpenCV on Raspberry Pi. There are some other libraries that allow you to perform tasks that are specific to computer vision, such as SimpleCV. In this chapter, we will go through the basics of SimpleCV and build a few basic applications for image/video processing. We will cover the following topics in this chapter:

- SimpleCV and its installation on Raspberry Pi
- The basics of image processing in SimpleCV
- The blurring effect on live video
- The green screen effect for still images

SimpleCV and its installation on Raspberry Pi

SimpleCV is an open source framework for Computer Vision applications. While using SimpleCV, you do not really have to worry about image formats, bit depths, and color spaces. You can get started with computer vision with SimpleCV with fewer lines of code as compared to OpenCV. SimpleCV is written in Python, and it's free to use. It runs on Mac, Windows, and Ubuntu Linux, and it is licensed under the BSD license.

Let's start our journey with the installation of SimpleCV on Pi.

Run the following command to install the necessary dependencies. You may have most of them installed on your Pi already:

```
sudo apt-get install ipython python-opencv python-scipy
python-numpy python-setuptools python-pip
```

Now, run the following command to install SimpleCV:

```
sudo pip install https://github.com/
  sightmachine/SimpleCV/zipball/master
```

Finally, run the following command to install the `svgwrite` dependency:

```
sudo pip install svgwrite
```

Pi is now ready for SimpleCV Programming. You can launch SimpleCV by typing `simplecv` on the terminal, as follows:

```
pi@pi02 ~ $ simplecv
```

This will take you to the SimpleCV interface, which is a line-oriented command interpreter:

```
+-----------------------------------------------------------+
 SimpleCV 1.3.0 [interactive shell] - http://simplecv.org
+-----------------------------------------------------------+

Commands:
  "exit()" or press "Ctrl+ D" to exit the shell
  "clear()" to clear the shell screen
  "tutorial()" to begin the SimpleCV interactive tutorial
  "example()" gives a list of examples you can run
  "forums()" will launch a web browser for the help forums
  "walkthrough()" will launch a web browser with a walkthrough

Usage:
  dot complete works to show library
  for example: Image().save("/tmp/test.jpg") will dot complete
  just by touching TAB after typing Image().

Documentation:
  help(Image), ?Image, Image?, or Image()? all do the same
  "docs()" will launch webbrowser showing documentation

SimpleCV:1>
```

You can exit the interface by typing the `exit()` command, which will bring you back to the OS command line. You can also follow the instructions under the commands section and explore it on your own. Rather than using SimpleCV in the interactive mode as shown previously, we will import SimpleCV into our Python scripts.

Getting started with the camera, display, and images

The following program will get us started with the camera and display. Make sure that a webcam is connected to Raspberry Pi before running the code:

```
# Program to take a picture using Webcam and display it on screen
from SimpleCV import Camera,Image,Display
import time
#Initialize the Display and Camera
disp=Display()
cap=Camera()

#Take a picture
image=cap.getImage()
#Show the picture on screen
image.save(disp)
time.sleep(5)
```

This simple program initialized the camera and display by using `cap=Camera()` and `disp=Display()` respectively. The `cap.getImage()` function captures an image from the `camera` and `image.save(disp)` displays it on the screen. The `time.sleep(5)` function waits for 5 seconds before the program terminates. The output of the preceding code is as follows:

The following program captures a live stream from the webcam and displays it on the screen:

```
from SimpleCV import *
cap=Camera()
cap.live()
```

If the camera is pointed to the display, you will see an interesting mirror effect, as follows:

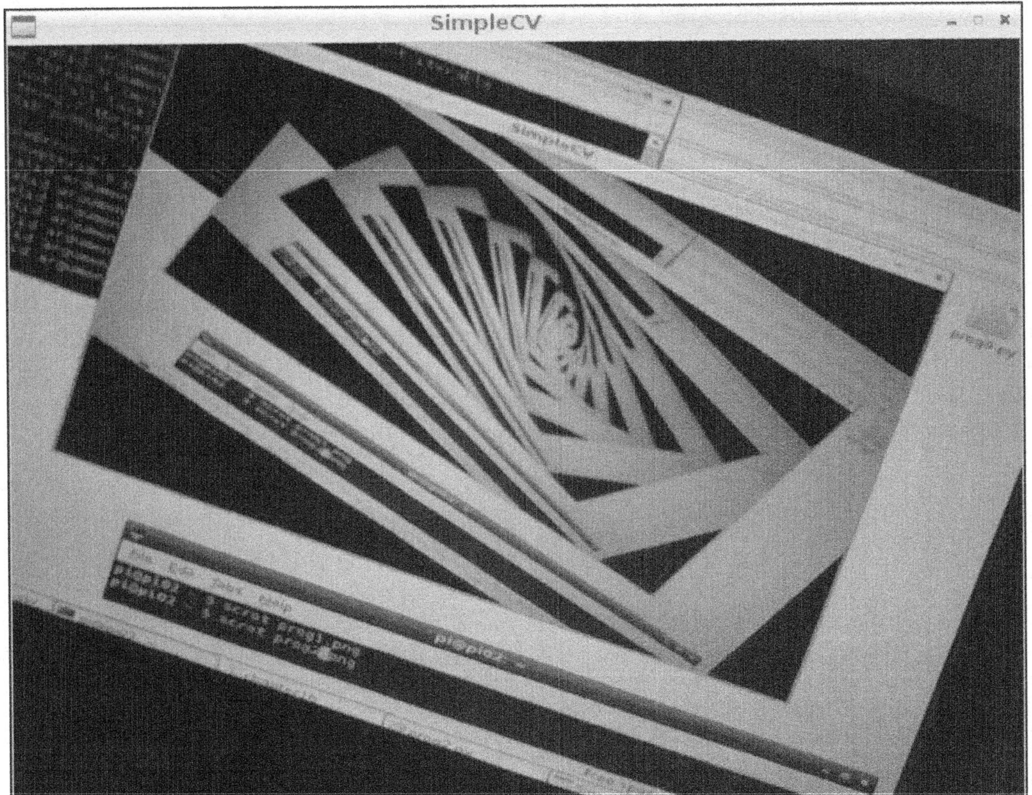

SimpleCV also has functions to read and display images from a specific location, just like OpenCV. It also contains inbuilt images within its library. The following program demonstrates these functionalities:

```
from SimpleCV import Image
import time

img= Image('/home/pi/book/test_set/1.5.01.tiff')
img.show()
```

```
time.sleep(5)

img=Image('logo')
img.show()
time.sleep(5)

img=Image('logo_inverted')
img.show()
time.sleep(5)

img=Image('lenna')
img.show()
time.sleep(5)
```

In the preceding program, `img= Image('/home/pi/book/test_set/1.5.01.tiff')` is used to read an image from a particular location, while `Image('logo')`, `img=Image('logo_inverted')`, and `img=Image('lenna')` are used to read the inbuilt images within the SimpleCV library. Run the preceding code and check out its output.

Binary thresholding and color distances

SimpleCV comes with the `binarize()` function, which converts an image into black and white (that is, it binarizes it). If we pass a numeric value between 0 and 255 to the `binarize()` function, then the value acts as a threshold. Otherwise, it uses Otsu's method for binarization. The following code demonstrates the usage of this function:

```
from SimpleCV import Image
import time
img = Image('logo')
otsu = img.binarize()
otsu.show()
time.sleep(5)
bin = img.binarize(127)
bin.show()
time.sleep(5)
```

Next, we will have a look at how to use the preceding function for image segmentation along with `colorDistance()`. The `colorDistance()` function calculates the distance between every pixel in an image and a given RGB color value. This function takes the RGB color as an argument, and it returns an image representing the distance from the specified color.

Let's have a step-by-step look at the code to retrieve a segment with a specific color from the image. The following code loads and displays the source image:

```
from SimpleCV import Image
import time

img1 = Image('/home/pi/book/test_set/4.1.03.tiff')
img1.show()
time.sleep(5)
```

The source image will be displayed as follows:

We want to extract the green segment from the image. We will use the `colorDistance()` function for this purpose, as follows (we will pass the RGB value of the green color in the image to this function):

```
greendist=img1.colorDistance((108,139,133))
```

Let's binarize and invert the preceding output, as follows:

```
greendistbin=greendist.binarize(30).invert()
greendistbin.show()
time.sleep(5)
```

The output will be as follows:

If we subtract this from the original image, we will be able to extract the green segment from the image:

```
onlygreen = img1 - greendistbin
onlygreen.show()
time.sleep(5)
```

The output will be as follows:

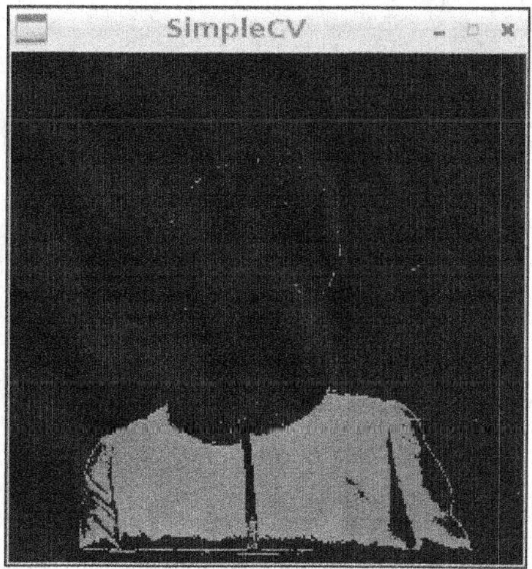

The blur effect on a live web camera feed

Let's write some code for visual effects. We can introduce a movie type blur effect to the live camera feed by a weighted addition of current and subsequent frames, as follows:

```
from SimpleCV import Camera, Display

cam=Camera()
WeightFactor=0.5
t0=cam.getImage()

disp=Display((t0.size()))

while not disp.isDone():
  t1=cam.getImage()
  img= (t1*WeightFactor)+(t0*(1-WeightFactor))
  img.save(disp)
  t0=t1
```

In the preceding code, we multiplied the current image with `WeightFactor` and multiplied the previous frame with (`1- WeightFactor`). Then, we added and displayed these weighted frames. This code works best against a still background and a single moving object. The output is as follows:

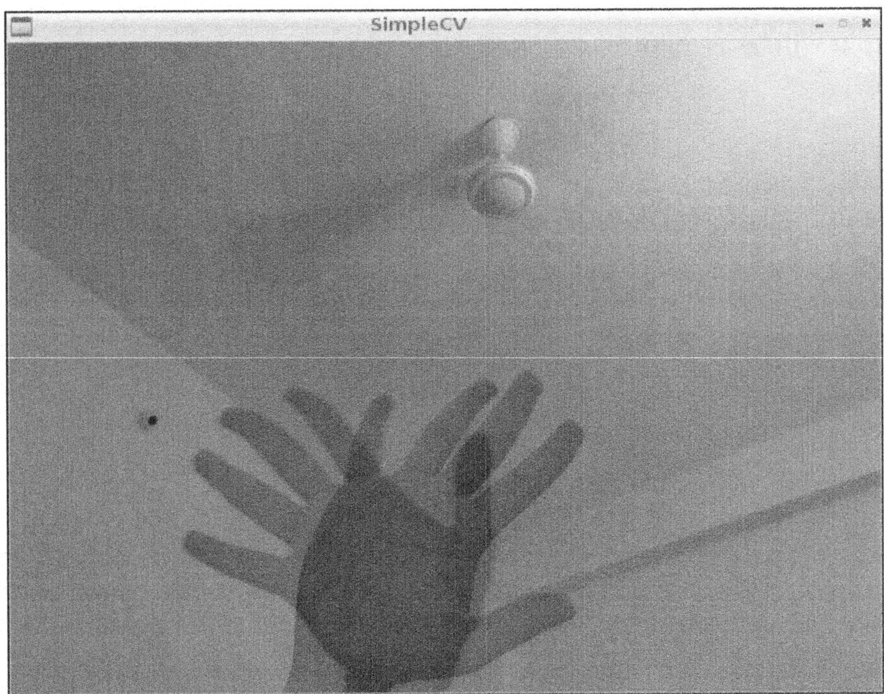

As an exercise, try changing the weights of the frames and compare the output.

Histogram calculation

The following example shows how to split an image into the individual RGB color channels and calculate the channel-wise color histogram:

```
from SimpleCV import Image
from matplotlib import pyplot as plt

img = Image('/home/pi/book/test_set/4.2.06.tiff')

(r,g,b)=img.splitChannels(False)

plt.subplot(311)
plt.plot(r.histogram(255),color='r')
plt.title('Red Histogram')
plt.xlim([0,256]), plt.yticks([])

plt.subplot(312)
plt.plot(g.histogram(255),color='g')
plt.title('Green Histogram')
plt.xlim([0,256]), plt.yticks([])

plt.subplot(313)
plt.plot(b.histogram(255),color='b')
plt.title('Blue Histogram')
plt.xlim([0,256]), plt.yticks([])

plt.show()
```

The color channel-wise histogram will be as follows:

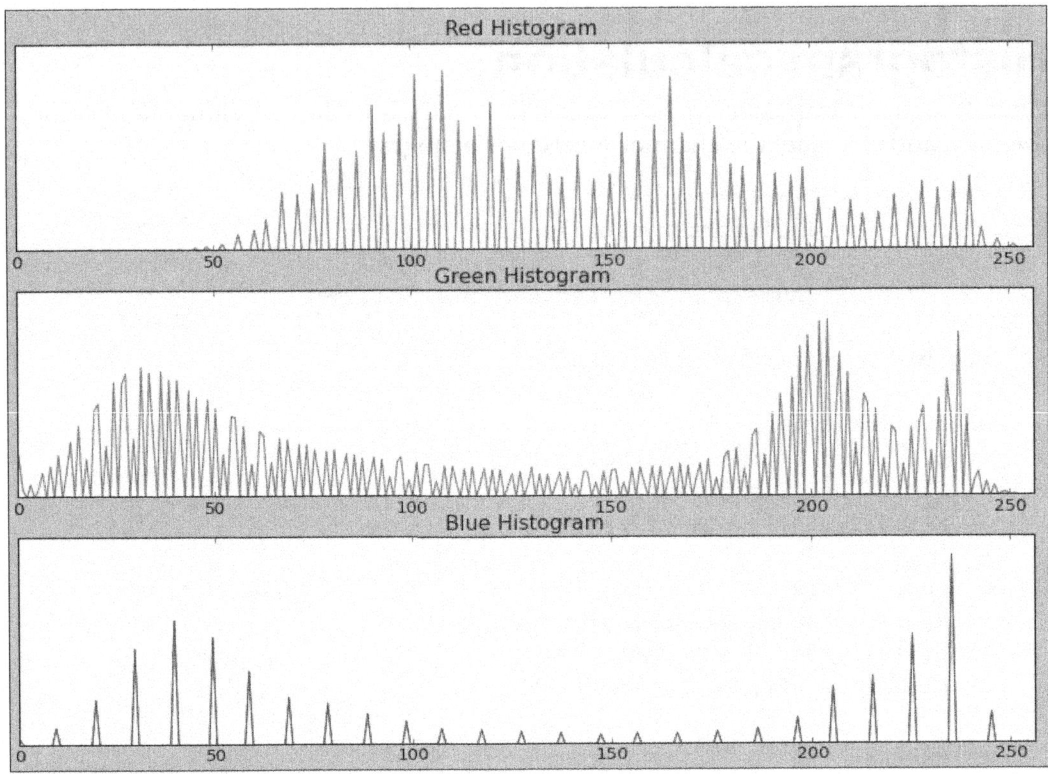

Greyscale conversion

An image can be converted to grayscale, as follows:

```
from SimpleCV import Image
import time
img=Image('/home/pi/book/test_set/4.2.05.tiff')
img.show()
time.sleep(5)
img.grayscale().show()
time.sleep(5)
```

Detecting corners and lines in an image

SimpleCV has the `findCorners()` and `findLines()` functions to detect the corners and lines in an image.

The following code is an example that demonstrates the usage of the `findCorners()` function:

```
from SimpleCV import Image
import time
img=Image('/home/pi/book/test_set/1.5.01.tiff')
img.grayscale().findCorners().show()
time.sleep(5)
```

The following code is an example that illustrates the usage of the `findLines()` function:

```
img=Image('/home/pi/book/test_set/1.5.01.tiff')
lines=img.findLines()
lines.draw(width=3)
img.show()
```

The output of the two preceding code will be as follows:

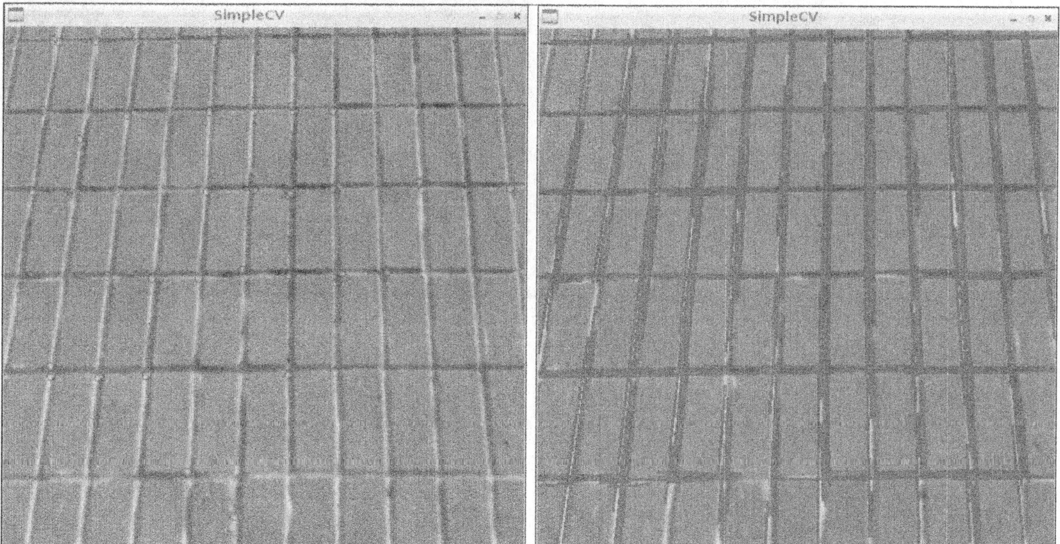

Blob detection in images

SimpleCV has functions to detect blobs in an image. The following code uses the `findBlobs()` function to detect blobs in the image:

```
from SimpleCV import Image
import time
img=Image('/home/pi/book/test_set/7.1.02.tiff')
imgBin=img.binarize()
blobs=imgBin.findBlobs()
blobs.show(width=5)
time.sleep(5)
```

The input image (an aerial photograph of a plane in a hanger) and the detected blobs are as follows:

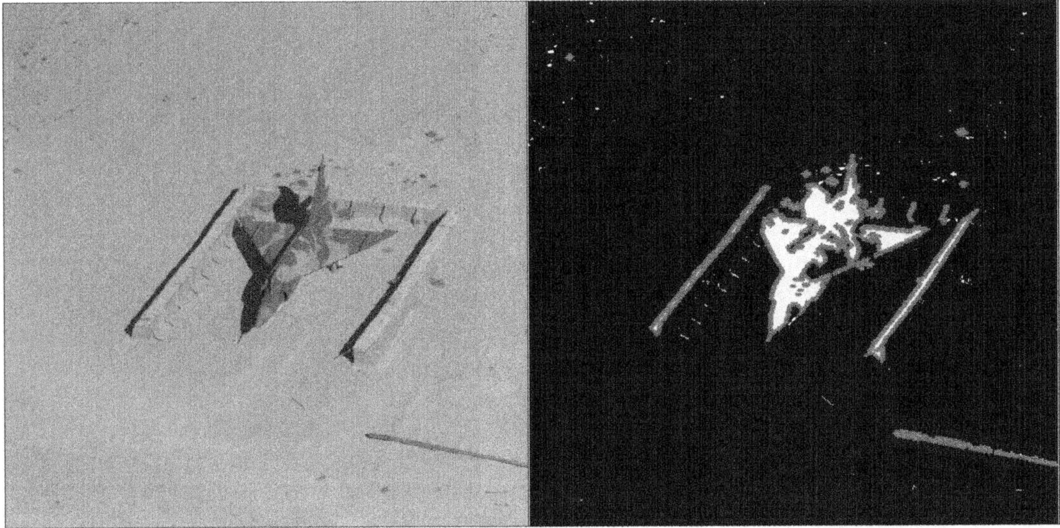

SimpleCV also has a `findSkintoneBlobs()` function that automatically finds skin-toned blobs from an image. The following program uses the `findSkintoneBlobs()` function on the live stream that is received from the camera:

```
from SimpleCV import Image, Camera

cam = Camera()
```

```
while 1:
  img=cam.getImage()
  skin =img.findSkintoneBlobs()

  if skin:
    for i in skin:
      print i.centroid()
    skin.draw(), skin.show()
  else:
    print "No Skin detected"
```

In the preceding program, we printed the centroids of the detected skin-toned blobs. However, the output is highly dependent on the skin tone of the subject person and the lighting conditions.

Sending Raspberry Pi on a boating vacation

We made Pi work a lot until now. Let's send it on a well-deserved boating vacation. We are going to achieve it by applying a chroma key (green screen) effect to a picture of Pi with a scenic image as a background. First, we will load and display Pi with a green background:

```
from SimpleCV import *
import time

print 'Displaying Candidate Image'
candidate = Image ('/home/pi/book/test_set/mypy.png')
candidate.show()
time.sleep(3)
```

This image is as follows:

Then, we will load and display the scenic lake background by using the following code:

```
print 'Displaying Background Image'
lake = Image ('/home/pi/book/test_set/lake.tif')
lake.show()
time.sleep(7)
```

The scenic lake background will be displayed as follows:

Then, we will calculate the hue distance with `hueDistance()`, and green as the hue color, and binarize it with the following code:

```
print 'Apply and display mask'
mask=candidate.hueDistance(color=Color.GREEN).binarize()
mask.show()
time.sleep(7)
```

This will create a binary mask with Raspberry Pi as a black area and the remainder as the white area, as follows:

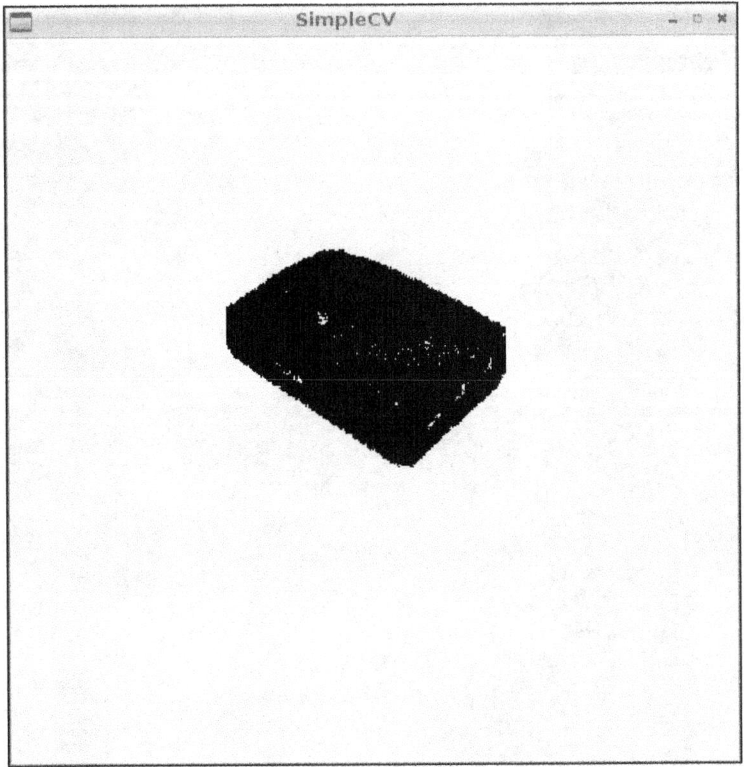

Finally, the following piece of code will create the necessary chroma key effect and send Pi on a boating vacation:

```
print 'Chroma Key Effect'
output=(lake - mask.invert()) + (candidate-mask)
output.show()
time.sleep(7)
```

For a better understanding, you may want to check the output of (`lake - mask.invert()`) and (`candidate-mask`) individually. The final output will be as follows:

You might want to implement the same on a live camera feed, just like we did in the previous chapter with OpenCV.

Exercise

You can visit `http://simplecv.org/`, the SimpleCV homepage, to explore the SimpleCV library in detail.

Summary

In this chapter, we explored the SimpleCV library for computer vision and wrote a few sample programs that demonstrated its power.

Congratulations! You have now completed reading the book.

While exploring the complex image processing and computer vision concepts, you discovered that Pi is an amazing little platform that can bring your ideas to life. Working through several challenging projects, you incrementally developed your expertise as a Computer Vision enthusiast by using open source tools, applications, and scripts.

Now, the real road lies ahead. You can use the knowledge and skills you acquired to build innovative project designs with high complexity and functionality.

Index

A

B

C

D

F

G

H

I

R

S

T

Thank you for buying
Raspberry Pi Computer Vision Programming

About Packt Publishing

Packt, pronounced 'packed', published its first book, *Mastering phpMyAdmin for Effective MySQL Management*, in April 2004, and subsequently continued to specialize in publishing highly focused books on specific technologies and solutions.

Our books and publications share the experiences of your fellow IT professionals in adapting and customizing today's systems, applications, and frameworks. Our solution-based books give you the knowledge and power to customize the software and technologies you're using to get the job done. Packt books are more specific and less general than the IT books you have seen in the past. Our unique business model allows us to bring you more focused information, giving you more of what you need to know, and less of what you don't.

Packt is a modern yet unique publishing company that focuses on producing quality, cutting-edge books for communities of developers, administrators, and newbies alike. For more information, please visit our website at `www.packtpub.com`.

About Packt Open Source

In 2010, Packt launched two new brands, Packt Open Source and Packt Enterprise, in order to continue its focus on specialization. This book is part of the Packt Open Source brand, home to books published on software built around open source licenses, and offering information to anybody from advanced developers to budding web designers. The Open Source brand also runs Packt's Open Source Royalty Scheme, by which Packt gives a royalty to each open source project about whose software a book is sold.

Writing for Packt

We welcome all inquiries from people who are interested in authoring. Book proposals should be sent to `author@packtpub.com`. If your book idea is still at an early stage and you would like to discuss it first before writing a formal book proposal, then please contact us; one of our commissioning editors will get in touch with you.

We're not just looking for published authors; if you have strong technical skills but no writing experience, our experienced editors can help you develop a writing career, or simply get some additional reward for your expertise.

Learning Raspberry Pi

ISBN: 978-1-78398-282-0 Paperback: 258 pages

Unlock you creative programming potential by creating web technologies, image processing, electronics- and robotics-based projects using the Raspberry Pi

1. Learn how to create games, web, and desktop applications using the best features of the Raspberry Pi.

2. Discover the powerful development tools that allow you to cross-compile your software and build your own Linux distribution for maximum performance.

Raspberry Pi Cookbook for Python Programmers

ISBN: 978-1-84969-662-3 Paperback: 402 pages

Over 50 easy-to-comprehend tailor-made recipes to get the most out of the Raspberry Pi and unleash its huge potential using Python

1. Install your first operating system, share files over the network, and run programs remotely.

2. Unleash the hidden potential of the Raspberry Pi's powerful Video Core IV graphics processor with your own hardware accelerated 3D graphics.

Please check **www.PacktPub.com** for information on our titles

CPSIA information can be obtained at www.ICGtesting.com
Printed in the USA
LVOW03s1326260815
451615LV00022B/290/P